"*This book brings a clarity of thought in how to make effective change in one's life. A must read.*"

–**Michael Appleton, Author,** *Dialogues to Success*

"*In Living the Big Picture, Vanora Spreen has done a great job of helping people identify their real barriers to success. She lays out some wonderful examples of how to live the good life!*"

—**Brian Buffini, Chairman/Founder of Buffini & Company, Co-Author of** *Work by Referral...Live the Good Life.*'

LIVING
THE
BIG PICTURE

LIVING
THE
BIG PICTURE

—One Promise at a Time—

By

VANORA SPREEN

DEDICATION

This book is dedicated to my husband Ken,
and my three (now adult) children, Darryl, Kristian
and Robbie. Each of you, in your own special way,
has taught me about life, love and understanding,
and through these lessons, myself. You have blessed
me in immeasurable ways. For all this and what is
yet to come, I am truly grateful.

Quantity discounts are available on bulk orders.
Contact sales@TAGPublishers.com for more information.

TAG Publishing, LLC
2618 S. Lipscomb
Amarillo, TX 79109
www.TAGPublishers.com

Office (806) 373-0114
Fax (806) 373-4004
info@TAGPublishers.com

ISBN: 978-1-59930-397-0

First Edition

Copyright © 2011 Vanora Spreen

Text: Lloyd Arbour, www.tablloyd.com

TABLE OF CONTENTS

ACKNOWLEDGEMENT

I want to express my immense gratitude for the many coaches and mentors I have had the privilege of working with and learning from over the years. It is said behind every great athlete, you will find an even better coach. I don't consider myself to be an athlete, but I do understand the sentiment. I have had the good fortune to have been coached and mentored by a number of great people including, Patti Marra, Dan Sullivan, James Ray, Raymond Aaron, Mike Ferry, Brian Buffini, Anthony Robbins, Paul Martinelli and Mary Morrissey. Of all my coaches and mentors, Bob Proctor has made a huge impact on my journey of self-discovery. He is not only my personal mentor. Bob has become my business partner. I would be remiss if I left out my writing coach, Kyle Word (no kidding – that's his real name!). Kyle has been so much fun to work with and also share some interesting pieces of trivia!

Of course, the Real Estate Community has been very good to me, offering me so many opportunities to make a difference in my clients' as well as other sales people's daily lives. In particular, I am grateful for my friendship with Bob Nutbrown and his ability to see in me what I didn't see in myself.

I have had many friends along my personal journey who have supported me through thick and thin and allowed me to grow in awareness *and* at my own speed! I include my sorority sisters in Beta Sigma Phi, in particular Iota Kappa Chapter – Brampton, Ontario in this wonderful group of people. Not only have we shared quite a few laughs, we have shed a few tears together as well.

Special mention, (in alphabetical order!) goes to Brenda, Cindy, Dean, Dittie, Donna, Karen, Marta, Michael, and Wolfgang. All of you have been a huge support in your own unique ways!

Of course, my sister Vicky, my husband Ken, my now grown children, Darryl, Kristian and Robbie have been my guiding lights – always there to hear my ideas and bounce things off. In particular I want to mention my youngest son Robbie. Rob, maybe you haven't realized that you are the reason I have written this book. You have been such an inspiration to me and in fact you are the person who prompted me to set out on my own journey of self-discovery. Together we have experienced some real highs and lows, and I am proud to say that I never doubted your incredible potential, even when things were difficult between us.

And now, as my teacher, Mary Morrissey would say, "All this or something better!"

FOREWORD

Living the Big Picture is where all human achievement begins. It is your emotional involvement with that picture that will enable you to either go through or around the road blocks that will inevitably pop up at the most unexpected moments as you're moving toward the materialization of your dream. It is the psychic medication that will relieve the pain you experience when you encounter rejection. Having a clear view of the *Big Picture* is an absolute prerequisite for success in every endeavor.

Vanora Spreen has done a magnificent job of charting a course for every person who truly seeks success. By following the path she has laid out before you and giving the time and attention it will require to create the promises to yourself that she has suggested, you will one day experience what Henry David Thoreau suggested when he said that *"You will meet with success unexpected in common hours."*

I have had the good fortune of knowing the author for some time. She has earned my admiration and my respect, and I can assure you the lessons that will unfold as you move from page to page are not fancy theories that she created while day dreaming or merely passing time, but are in fact well-earned lessons of an extremely successful lady.

In writing this book, Vanora Spreen would appear to have followed the strategy of a professional astronomer as she went back and charted the course she herself had followed, tracking all the major moves and lessons she learned and has so eloquently shared with each of us who are fortunate enough to hold this wonderful book in the palm of our hands.

I encourage you to treat Vanora's book as a guide, following each lesson meticulously. By doing so, day in and day out, you will find that what you're holding in your hands will magically turn into some form of a *Global Positioning System* that will lead you to the door step of any goal you choose to set for yourself.

Before approaching the fundamental principles upon which this book is founded, it will be of benefit to you to keep in mind the fact that it is practical, that it brings you to the discoveries of many years of research, research that the author has done for you.

The personal growth that Vanora outlines in the first chapter is really the great reward for the time and energy you devote to the application of all the various principles she covers in future chapters. Personal growth is the ultimate reward. Please keep in mind you are merely a custodian. Everything you own at the time of your passing will belong to someone else. But what you are is yours forever.

As you pass from the first to the second chapter, I want to recommend that Purpose is truly the glue that holds everything together and makes all the coming chapters meaningful. This chapter will require your time and your undivided attention. Don't rush it. But rather be calm and take your time.

Your purpose is something you will discover. Permit me to quote a mentor of mine – Napoleon Hill –

"It is impressive to recognize that all of the great leaders, in all walks of life and during all periods of history, have attained their leadership by the application of their abilities behind a definite major purpose. It is no less impressive to observe that those who are classified as failures have no such purpose, but they go around and around, like a ship without a rudder, coming back always empty-handed, to their starting point."

By effectively following the suggestions given to you in the second chapter, you would find it easy and in fact pleasurable to turn each of the subjects covered in the following chapters into stepping stones to move you higher, to elevate your consciousness, to create a greater awareness, and in doing so you will feel as if you were focusing a pair of binoculars as you begin to see the Big Picture with a clarity you have never before experienced.

–Sandra Gallagher
President/CEO
LifeSuccess Productions, LLC

INTRODUCTION

Living The Big Picture

Have you ever watched artists at work? Seen how they seem to focus with laser-like intensity on a minute portion of their painting or sculpture, and then take a step back to put things in perspective?

My daughter, Kristian is an artist. I have watched how she goes over every little detail of her work with an intensity of focus that I truly admire. Then she takes a step back to look at the whole, to look at the big picture. She may then decide that it is perfect just the way it is, or she may decide to make some adjustments, add a little more colour, lighten things up, add some shadow, change the focus, look at the balance of colour, and the list goes on!

It was while watching her paint one day that I realized that we can take the same approach in our day-to-day lives. Focus on a minute detail, make a decision and then act upon our decision. But this may be where the similarity ends. How many of us really examine the outcomes of our decisions in terms of our "big picture"? How many of us take the time to create a "big picture" in the first place? How many of us recognize that the decisions we make in one area of our life affect the others? Now we see the crux of the problem. Many of us are making decisions without regard to the adverse affects we are creating for ourselves, our relationships, our businesses, and our most precious resource—our health. We get caught up in the minute details, ignoring the giant elephant in the room.

Looking back over my own life, I now realize the many decisions that I have made without really considering my long-term dreams or desires, focusing instead on things that I perceived at the time to be the immediate payback. Sometimes these things worked out, sometimes they didn't. Sometimes an unexpected turn of events (in other words, an unexpected outcome) really set me back a few paces.

And still other times, just plain poor decisions, based on confused or opposing values, triggered regrets and missed opportunities. I remember a conversation with my broker, when I was new to the real estate industry, about there being times when I would have to choose between my family and my business. I remember thinking that idea was crazy! Of course I would choose my family. That is, until the time came when another family's plans became more important than my own.

Experience is the best teacher, and from experience, knowledge and wisdom are born! I had to learn a few lessons the hard way. So my journey began, questioning my values and what was truly important to me. What did I want for myself and my family? What did I want my legacy to be?

Of course, I have had some wonderful mentors and teachers along my path who have helped me in immeasurable ways; for this I am truly grateful. So, it is in this spirit that I hope to convey to you just how important it is to take that step back every now and then. Become the artist. Create in your mind's eye a wonderful vision for your life. Begin to live your vision. Then, take that step back again, evaluate, put things in perspective, and paint your next stroke!

CHAPTER ONE
—Time For A Stretch—

CHAPTER ONE

—*Time For A Stretch*—

*Why am I so unhappy and disappointed in so
many parts of my life?*
Why isn't my life the way I wished it would be?
Why isn't the world the way I want it?
Is this all there is?

A large number of unhappy people ask themselves
questions like these every day. Whether it's peace on earth, a
great job, or a great relationship, they simply don't seem to get
what they think they want. Their personal lives, their business
and professional lives, their finances and their relationships
simply don't bring them the happiness that they ought to enjoy.

Think about it. In your personal life, are you satisfied? You
live in a particular house or apartment, in a neighborhood, in
a town or city. You may live alone or with one or more family
members or with a significant other. You may have pets. Each
one of these factors has multiple facets, any one of which can
be unsatisfactory to you.

Your home may be larger or smaller than you like. Your
yard (or lack of a yard) may be a problem for you. How are
your neighbours? Do you enjoy their company? Do you even
know your neighbours' *names*?

Obviously, very few of us have every single aspect of our
lives lined up in a tidy row of perfection. There are always
things in our lives that can be improved upon. Sometimes,

though, we feel a deep unhappiness and discontent with the way things have worked out. Those thoughts can begin to take over, making you unable to enjoy the many things in your personal life that are right.

Take a look at your professional life. You may work for someone else, or you may be self-employed. Are you happy at what you're doing? Is it something you imagined doing as a child? Do you feel you are making a contribution, or are you just putting in time? Do you derive a sense of accomplishment and fulfillment from your work, or is it simply a way to pay the bills?

Sadly, many—if not most—people exist in what Henry David Thoreau called, "lives of quiet desperation." They go through each day enduring everything from extreme misery to vague discontent. Happiness is an abstract idea to these folks. The bigger pity is that they could transform their lives for the better if they were only willing to make changes.

Why don't people make the changes necessary to improve their lives? The answer is both simple and complex. Human beings are held back by fear.

Fear is one of the most primal emotions we have. It's what made it possible for our caveman ancestors to survive. Thousands of years ago, sticking your head out of your cave invited the real possibility that you would wind up as some savage beast's dinner. The cavemen that didn't feel enough fear ventured out and never came back.

Most of us are fortunate enough not to be in a situation where a saber-toothed tiger will snack on us. However, we are still wired the same way as our ancestors were. A new or unknown situation still provokes a fearful response in us. Ask anyone who has been asked to "say a few words" to an audience about how intensely fear can grab you. The heart beats faster, the stomach churns, and it suddenly becomes very difficult to breathe.

With our circuitry designed to preserve us in the face of the unknown, we instinctively avoid anything that might carry damage or a penalty. As a result, we sit in our caves and endure whatever pains or discomforts might assail us, because what is outside might be worse. And so, we live in quiet desperation rather than taking a chance to improve the situation.

It's the simplest thing in the world to avoid making a life-altering decision, whether it's to change jobs, move to another city or even find a new significant other. We rationalize our decision to do nothing like experts—we can justify that decision in very creative ways. Meanwhile, we simply accept and endure what life throws at us.

When we tell ourselves false stories to rationalize staying where we are, we fool our minds. The body, however, tries to tell us the truth. We suffer from anxiety, stress, depression and any number of mental, emotional and physical ailments. One of the greatest causes of disease in modern society is simply worry.

Every year some organization lists the greatest fears that people have, from the fear of death to the fear of public speaking. What most of us are really afraid of, though, is *change*. Our caveman instincts do everything they can to maintain the status quo.

The comfortable thing with keeping things just the way they are is that you don't have to explain yourself. If you start trying to make big changes to your life, even to improve it, friends and family start asking questions. They may even encourage you to "leave well enough alone"—not understanding that you are not feeling "well" enough. You may not feel well at all.

Of course, when we're talking about change and the fear it causes, we have to mention the fear of the unknown. Many people experience fear bordering on panic when confronted by a snake or a spider. Yet these creatures are studied and held in high regard by other people. Is it reasonable to figure that if we knew more about snakes we would be less afraid of them?

Our ignorance is often the most limiting factor. Ignorance is *not knowing*. By definition, if we feel a change is necessary, we can't know with absolute certainty what the future will bring. We can give it a measured, reasonable guess, but we can't know for sure. That not knowing is often enough to stimulate our fear and to hold us back.

Whenever we want to make a change, we often give other factors undue importance. We may worry about what people will say, or what people will think. Each January, when newspaper and magazine articles are filled with ideas on setting New Year's resolutions, it is often recommended to publicly announce your resolutions to friends and family. This supposedly motivates you to try harder and to gain their support in your endeavor.

While the suggestion has merit, it also carries with it the chance of stigma: *What will people think if I don't hit the goal I set for myself?* That thought alone can paralyze someone who is sensitive to other people's opinions. The idea of change, and how other people will perceive them, frightens many people.

Another reason to be cautious in sharing your ideas about change with others is that they may resist your desire to change. Friends and family may not want you to change for their own self-interested reasons. They may feel that you will move away from them, emotionally or physically. They may worry about the potential loss of your friendship or the close personal connection you have with them. It may also be out of guilt, as your focus on improvement will remind them of their own shortcomings. Many, if not most people, are satisfied with the status quo.

Whenever we make some sort of change—whether to change jobs, move to another city, even drop a bad habit—the change that we are really achieving is a change in our *self image*. In other words, you may *see yourself* as an apartment dweller, so the prospect of moving to a house and taking on a mortgage frightens you. You may *see yourself* as a fat person, so going on a diet to lose weight makes you nervous.

What's funny about our self image is that it may not even be accurate. Plenty of adults who were chubby as children grow out of it and become slender. Many of them, however, still see themselves as that pudgy adolescent, and set themselves up for a roller coaster ride of weight gain and weight loss, trying one diet and exercise plan after another.

Even if we recognize that fear of change is holding us back, we sometimes still allow it to have power over us. As mentioned earlier, we can rationalize any decision we make, and it will seem sensible on some level. Very few of us can be truly objective when it comes to explaining why we don't improve our lives.

Mostly the cause is that we hold on to beliefs that were developed early in our lives. Often these beliefs were based on faulty information. Nonetheless, they still hold power over us. We wind up telling ourselves stories to rationalize why we don't change. See if any of these statements strike a chord:

- If I change, I'll run into a new situation that I'm not ready for. I might fail, and I'll look stupid.
- If I change, I'll be stressed and uncomfortable all the time.
- If I change, it tells the world I've done something wrong or bad, or that I'm inadequate.
- If I change, I'll expose myself to danger.

When we read the words on plain paper like this, they don't seem to have much power. Intellectually, we know that they are almost all based on false premises. Emotionally, however, we feel the truth behind the statements. The belief systems that guide us do so through our emotions. We may know something is false, yet emotionally, we believe it.

You can look at change as almost the bizarre opposite of certain clichés. For example, we've all heard the saying, "the grass is always greener on the other side of the fence," implying that we perceive what someone else has as better than what we have. Ironically, even if we really believe the saying, we are too frightened to cross the fence to check out the grass. There might be something scary there.

You can always use the fear of failure as an excuse not to change. This is one of the excuses that really falls apart when examined intellectually, but which holds you in its grip emotionally. Of course you might fail if you try something new. For even the most talented and brilliant people, however, repeatedly trying and failing, and *then trying again,* is the standard way to progress toward excellence. What's more, even if you don't hit your original goal, you likely will improve in the particular area you're working on. Refusing to try something new because you might fail is rejecting one of the most effective tools to improvement that human beings possess.

PERSONAL GROWTH

After we recognize the existence of the fears that hold us back, what do we do? They seem to hold such power over us. What are the steps to making the changes we need to make so as to improve our lives?

First of all, we have to emotionally accept that the possibility of a better life exists. This is sometimes the most difficult task for those who are seriously depressed. They believe that their lives will *always* be miserable, or that things will *never* get better. It's a tragic paradox that those who need to make changes the most are often the most resistant to seeing the possibility of change.

Personal growth is the process of emphasizing the possible rather than the impossible. Your life reflects what you most focus on. When you focus on improving your life, then you will see more and more avenues open to you. New opportunities, new ways of thinking, and seemingly random events will present themselves. At times, such occurrences can seem almost magical. The reality, however, is that simply by paying attention to the various resources you have available makes new resources more clear.

This particular situation is not unusual. Have you ever decided to buy something new, say, a particular make and model of new car, and suddenly see that type of car everywhere? It's not that similar cars magically appear. It's the fact that your attention is guided to them by your interest in the specifics.

Personal growth is the process of living a fulfilling life. Fulfillment happens in different ways, and means different things to different people. Although each of us is an individual, we each recognize when we are doing the most with the talents and attributes we are given. We know when we have rewarding relationships with other people.

It is when we work to maximize that fulfillment that we experience personal growth. It's living in the moment, in the *now,* and doing our best at whatever task or chore is directly in front of us. There is almost a mystical Zen aura attached to such thoughts, but there doesn't have to be. Merely by selecting the right things to do, then doing them in the right ways to the best of our abilities, we are growing as human beings.

When we talk about personal growth, we are of course talking about *positive* change. The metaphor of "growth" is used consciously, as a plant works its way upward toward the light. Many people mistake increased abilities or talents for license to manipulate or abuse other people. What such people fail to realize, though, is that there are always consequences for one's actions. Positive growth brings positive consequences. The opposite also holds true.

MOTIVATORS

Fundamentally, human beings are motivated by only two things—pain and pleasure. A healthy individual moves toward pleasure and avoids pain. As simple as that sounds, it brings with it very complex challenges regarding why we do the things we do.

As mentioned earlier, we are ruled by our emotions. What happens, then, when we engage in an activity that we know is bad for us? Many people ask themselves, *Why do I do what I know I shouldn't do?*

The answer is this: everything we do, on at least some level, brings us pleasure that outweighs any accompanying pain. The smoker may view himself as a rebel living outside the normal rules of society. That's quite a romantic image. To quit smoking would mean giving up that image and becoming just like everyone else. Emotionally, the pleasure at being perceived (at least in his own mind) as a romantic rebel is greater than the pain of knowing that smoking can kill him.

All of our decisions work in the same way. We have, sometimes, mysterious motivations that cause us to experience pleasure from things in our lives that by any rational measure are not pleasurable. The conclusion, then, is that our emotions are not rational. They function based on programming and experiences that cause a particular sensation.

When you're dealing with something irrational like your emotions, it sometimes takes a cataclysmic event to initiate change. There are many heart patients in hospitals who are forced to change their lifestyles because their previous choices nearly killed them. Exercise, eating right, and getting more rest suddenly become very important when you've just been released from intensive care.

On the other side of the coin, there are times when an opportunity presents itself, and the struggle between the pain of change and the pain of missing an opportunity becomes intense. In a case like that, you might opt for the choice that you think will give you the least amount of pain. It's much healthier, of course, if you are drawn by the pleasure of what the opportunity can mean to your life. The choice is the same, even if the motivation is different.

Sometimes dissatisfaction with one's life becomes so unbearable that the desire to make a change is the driving force. This type of change doesn't have to be extremely painful, or even unhealthy. It can come from the realization that you're not doing enough with the talents, skills and other attributes you already possess. The desire to grow into one's abilities makes personal growth a very powerful force.

The truth is, you are going to have to change whether you want to or not. Your world will change regardless of what decisions you make. Those changes may be positive or they may be negative, but they *will* occur.

Whether through random natural events such as storms and earthquakes, or through other people's actions, things change around us. The economic turmoil in recent years has caused many people to make changes they were not ready for. A new business opening in your neighborhood can force changes onto your company.

STAGNATION

Stagnation is the determined effort to avoid change. Ponds stagnate when they don't have fresh water coming into them. The same water stays in the pond and the nutrients are slowly leached away by fish and other natural forces. The pond becomes unable to support life, and slowly, it dies. Without fresh water—change—to refresh it, any body of water will become stagnant.

We see something similar in people who refuse to change. They somehow become less alive. They may stay in the same position for a long time, never moving up because they are afraid to change. They are passed over for promotions and raises, and slowly sink to the bottom.

Companies can stagnate, too. Businesses that refuse to adapt to changing business conditions are almost guaranteed to go under. Technological advances, increased competition, changes in customer tastes—all of these demand change from a business that aspires to profit and prosper.

How do you avoid stagnation? You have to be willing to address the fear that you may feel at making changes. Knowing that the fear exists, and that it has no basis in reality, can be the first step in adjusting and adapting in ways that improve your life.

What this means is that you have to look for possibility in life. You have to grasp emotionally that you are in a position to do more, to have more, to accomplish more. Opportunities present themselves to people who are ready for them. You can put yourself in that position simply by changing your mental state.

What's the best way to experience growth? First of all, you have to be willing to dream big. Begin to stretch your mind to see new possibilities.

Add to your life as it is now. Not all change has to be earth-shaking. Simply add to the quality of your life as you currently live it. At the same time, look around and see if there are larger changes you can make that will improve it even more.

HOLISTIC CHANGE

I agree with many experts who recommend that we address changes in our lives *holistically*. A holistic outlook is one in which we consider the whole rather than simply the sum of the individual parts. When most of us see a car, we don't think of it as tires, an engine, steering wheel, mirrors, etc. We view the entire thing as a means of transportation. It gets us from one place to another.

Viewing change in your life holistically acknowledges that you are not simply one thing, and that your life has many aspects. Your relationships, your physical health, your finances—these are all parts of what make you *you*— but you are much more than those things and you certainly can't be accurately defined by any single aspect.

Retaining a holistic view is important because changes you make in one part of your life will inevitably have consequences in other parts of your life. If you decide to improve your physical health, the odds are good that you will also improve your emotional health. Feeling better physically may enable you to do more things with family and friends, improving your relationships. One simple decision begets multiple results. These are the kinds of factors to be considered as you make decisions.

A holistic view enables you to better keep a balanced perspective when you make decisions. Especially during times when we experience great emotion, our judgment can sometimes become faulty. Have you ever gotten excited when seeing an advertisement for something, and told yourself "I *have* to have one of those!" only to later regret your hasty decision to buy? (Full confession: I have.)

When you take time to view how your decisions will affect various parts of your life, you find yourself making better, more thought-out decisions. You may still go with your initial impulse—that new kitchen gadget may work for you—but at least you've given it proper consideration.

Looking at the whole of your life also makes you better able to accommodate the inevitable changes that life brings. A young married couple may be committed to working hard to improve their finances, devoting hours and energy to their careers. When a baby enters the picture, though, that affects many parts (if not *all* parts) of their lives, and they may need to change some of their earlier decisions based on their new situation.

After you've made the decision to see your life as a whole, the next question you have may be: How do I implement a holistic view? There are numerous ways, but here are just a few.

Setting goals. Sometimes we decide we want something, and set a "goal" to achieve it. In and of itself, that action is great. Between *deciding* and *setting*, however, is where we ask ourselves tough questions. At what cost does achieving the goal come? What return will I receive on the time and energy invested? Am I willing to experience an imbalance in my life to reach this goal?

Only you can answer these questions. Some goals are worth striving for, while others are not. The goal itself may be important, but the way you reach it may need to be adjusted to reduce the impact on other parts of your life. Most goals can be reached in multiple ways. The trick is to find the way that keeps the other parts of your life at their highest, most satisfying, levels.

Time. How you spend your time helps you define what you consider important. (I will always remember when it was suggested to me that a quick look at my schedule and chequebook would clearly indicate what it was that I valued!) The point is you are the one who decides to spend evenings studying or attending classes rather than watching television. You exercise half an hour each morning rather than lingering over your cup of coffee. You see one more client rather than visit with friends.

This is not to say that occasionally enjoying a relaxing moment is not important. Renewing your emotional batteries is a vital ingredient to a quality life. Holistically considering your life and how you spend it, however, helps you better plan your activities in a way that helps your overall wellbeing.

The truth is that sometimes we fall into activities that benefit us in very limited ways. Habit is a very powerful force, and when we consciously decide how we'll spend our time, rather than letting random activities dominate our day, we can benefit in multiple ways.

Evaluation. Ultimately, the best argument for a holistic view of life is that we are better able to evaluate our lives, our decisions, and our goals. While we have to live our lives moment to moment, where the "rubber meets the road," it helps to be aware of the entire map, to see if we're on the *right* road.

For example, using the example above, when the mother and father with the new baby evaluate their lives in a holistic way, they may realize that spending time together and with their child pays much greater dividends than trying to earn more money at their jobs. Whatever they decide, the best decision for them comes after they have looked at their big picture.

Ultimately, the process of growing and improving your life begins with looking within yourself. Everything you need to make your life better is already inside you. Willingness to take a look inside is the most important attribute you can have as someone on the journey to personal growth.

A WORD ABOUT PROMISES

Whether we call it a resolution, an oath, a covenant, a commitment or something else, deciding and committing to a course of action is the truest way to achieving a more successful and fulfilling life. As a child, my mom always cautioned me to 'only make promises that I intend to keep'. Making and keeping promises to other people establishes your integrity and increases your influence in their lives. You enhance your reputation as a quality individual.

Making and keeping promises to *yourself*, however, is key to implementing the changes that you want to make. It gives you confidence and belief in the power that you have in controlling your future. Consider carefully the promises you make, and then commit to them. You will be amazed at the positive benefits you will receive.

With that in mind, I will end each chapter of this book with promises that you can keep to yourself. No single one of them by itself is huge, but you will see a tremendous cumulative effect. Read these promises and recognize how much they can benefit you. In your own life, you will begin to realize the great power that making and keeping promises can have.

MY PROMISE

I promise...

- to read this book with an open heart and mind,
- to look deep within myself,
- to allow myself to dream,
- to uncover what it is I truly desire, and
- to determine what I want my life to be, have and mean.

CHAPTER TWO
—Living With Purpose—

CHAPTER TWO

— *Living With Purpose—*

In the previous chapter I talked about making changes in your life. If you've decided that you want to make changes, some of them may be big and obvious—*I'd like to lose some weight*—while others may be more subtle—*Why do I always feel sad?* In other words, you have to determine where you want to make changes, and what kind of changes you want to make. The best place to start with anything is at the beginning.

The beginning of the process of positive change is first of all deciding where you are. There are steps to this process, each of which you can take in turn. You accomplish the first step by asking yourself questions. There is a variety of questions that you ask yourself daily, from deciding what shoes you'll wear today to wondering if you should have that extra slice of birthday cake. These questions are mundane parts of everyday life.

What I have in mind is something much more momentous. Ultimately, the shoes you decide to wear won't affect your life very much, even though we know that shoes can make an outfit! To begin implementing changes in your life, start by asking yourself Big Questions.

Big Questions are the ones that sort of stun you when you try to answer them. For example, the question, *"What's important to me?"* can be answered many different ways, some of them depending only on what time of day it is. The best questions are those which require you to put some thought into the answer. You want to ask Big Important Questions.

Some possible questions are

- What is important to me?
- Who is important to me?
- When do I feel most alive?
- Why do I do the things I do?
- How do I want to spend my time?
- Where do I want my life to be in five years?
- Who are the important people in my life?

You'll note that these questions are Kipling's "honest serving-men" from his poem "The Elephant's Child" –

I have six honest serving-men
They taught me all I knew.
Their names are What and Why and When
And How and Where and Who.

(It sometimes helps to go back to the classics to help determine what's important.)

With Kipling's help, you can ask quality questions to determine what type of changes you want to make in your life. One caution, however. You can ask the best questions in the world, but unless you are scrupulously honest with your answers to these questions, your benefit will be limited.

You'll find that the quality of the questions you ask frequently corresponds to the quality of your life. In addition to the introspective questions posed above, think about the questions you ask other people. Are you asking them questions that allow an honest and forthright answer? Or are you asking questions with the intention of saying, "*Gotcha*"?

In the same way we can ask questions of ourselves (or of the Universe) that reinforce a weak or negative self image. *Why is this happening to me? Why am I so stupid, fat, lazy, dumb, etc.?*

It can help to ask questions that reflect the perspective of being able to control your own actions. *How can I learn from this? What part of this plan can be salvaged? How can I improve?*

These questions are a bit different and separate from the Big Questions I mentioned earlier, but effective questions are some of the best tools that you can have in your toolbox. If you think back on the questions you ask yourself—especially at emotionally charged moments—you'll see that your questions frequently need an upgrade.

With the Big Questions, it's sometimes difficult to come up with an answer. If a particular question challenges you, don't hesitate to get those closest to you to help you answer it. *What are my strongest assets?* may be tough for you to answer by yourself. Your family, friends and coworkers, however, will have a solid idea of how to answer such a question.

Each of us is blessed with a *unique strength*. That strength is something that differentiates us from every other human being. When you consider your own unique strength—and you may have more than one—use the knowledge of it to help determine your Purpose. Some more questions you can ask:

- What are my unique strengths?
- What do I need to do to utilize them more effectively?
- Do I have the mindset I need to continue to grow?
- What do I need to study to continue on my learning path?
- Am I prepared to invest both time and money into my personal development?

The point of all these questions is to help you recognize the important matters that determine your very first objective—your *Purpose*.

Every one of us is put on earth with a definite mission in mind. We have individual strengths, interests and qualities that make us unique. Along with those traits—or perhaps because of them—there is a specific Purpose for which we exist. There is one thing which we were simply born to do.

How do you recognize your Purpose? This will be where you can refer to your Big Important Questions to find the answer.

Sometimes you will recognize you are 'on purpose' when you are in the middle of things! On becoming a new manager, I had started coaching a particular sales person. I noticed a deep sense of fulfillment, a realization that I was experiencing joy and that somehow I had contributed to this person's success. I began to notice each time I had this experience.

Have you ever had a moment when everything seemed to be perfect for you? An instance when time seemed to stand still? When everything just seemed *right*?

Most people have too few of such occasions. Notice when you are engaged in an activity that absorbs you so much that you don't notice the passing of time. That may be an indication that you have found your Purpose.

It takes more than absorption, however, to determine that an activity is what you were born to do. Millions of teenagers are absorbed in the internet or their cell phones. Simply being distracted does not a Purpose make.

On top of that somewhat mystical moment of time standing still, you should also enjoy a deep sense of fulfillment when you do certain things. For example, you may spend time volunteering at a homeless shelter, or at a nursing home. Those occasions may pass quickly because of how rewarding the time is. Moreover, you experience a deep sense of fulfillment from your efforts.

Besides a sense of fulfillment and time standing still, what else can help you discover your Purpose? The biggest factor is the moment when you recognize that what you're doing simply *feels right*.

Although this may sound mystical and mysterious, it's common for us to experience moments of bliss when everything seems to be lined up just perfectly for us. It happens often enough that we have phrases such as "that strikes a chord" or everything is "in sync" to help us describe the experience. Although the experience is somewhat difficult to describe, and probably defies rigid scientific scrutiny, it's very real.

The most important thing to keep in mind is that such experiences don't depend on a temporary situation to happen. They tap into the core of our being, rather than reflect the moment's demands. Again, such moments are not mere distractions, but resonate with us in a special way.

It helps to take a moment during our reflections to help us determine how we got where we are. If you are at a point in your life where you would like to make some changes and experience personal growth, then you obviously want to make better or different decisions than you've made up until now. With that in mind, a Big Question to ask yourself is: How did I get where I am?

Pretend that your world is the ocean. The ocean is full of many different types of creatures, some large and some small.

In this scenario, you are one of the sea creatures—whether a whale or a shrimp depends on you! Besides all the other people/ sea creatures you contend with, you also have to contend with the tides and the currents of the ocean itself.

Many times we let the currents of life move us to and fro without any real direction. You may be working at a job that you don't particularly care for, simply because it was the first one for which you applied. You may be associating with people whom you met randomly.

Much of our lives happens accidentally. As a result, we obtain accidental consequences. We may live less happily than we could if we only took a little more control. By letting the world direct you, you wound up where you are now.

This apparent randomness is actually not random at all. You made decisions, either consciously or unconsciously, that resulted in your life as it is now. Although random events happen to everyone, the vast majority of adults make judgments and take actions that bring them to their current situation in life.

As with most things, some of the decisions were likely very good and others were not as good. If you understand and embrace the concept of cause and effect, then another question leaps naturally to mind. If I make better decisions, isn't it likely that my life could improve?

Although where you are does not determine where you can go, *how* you got there is vitally important. It is understanding the decisions we made previously, repeating the good ones, and improving (or eliminating) the poor ones, that make improvement and personal growth possible.

First, a couple of words about decisions and decision-making. Scientists and psychologists have spent many hours researching how people make decisions. I won't pretend to understand all the technical terms their papers have produced. What I do know, though, is that our decision-making process often boils down to making one of two choices.

We decide to do something because it will increase our pleasure.

We decide to do something because it will decrease our pain.

Even toddlers learn very early that something that is hot causes pain—"hot" is often one of the earliest words they learn. They also understand very young that sweets such as candy or fruit give them pleasure. Pain and pleasure are two concepts human beings understand at a very young age.

If you want to see how quickly we respond to such motivators, watch a toddler among a group of adults. If he does something cute, everyone laughs. This feedback gives him pleasure, and he repeats the action in hopes of getting more laughter. His decision was based on the pleasure he derived from the crowd.

As we get older, our choices become more complex. We often do things that are bad for us. Rationally, these things should cause us pain, meaning we would do less of them. However, people still continue to smoke cigarettes, overeat, spend too much money, and so on. How does that happen?

It's because we have learned to associate certain activities —even those that are bad for us—with pleasure. The action, therefore, gives us both pain *and* pleasure. Our normal decision-making circuitry gets short circuited.

Take overeating, for example. Western culture has produced more food than any time in history. As a result, westerners have adapted their eating habits to accommodate this increase in the food supply. Portion sizes are larger than they have ever been, and our waistlines reflect that.

For the last forty years or so, the media have made much of the increasing obesity problem confronting our culture, and, more recently, confronting our children. The bad things that happen to a person's health as a result of obesity are no secret. Rationally, that would make overeating a painful decision.

On the other hand, think of the emotions that we associate with food. During the holidays we get together with family and friends, celebrate, and have a good time… around the dinner table. Turkey dinner at Thanksgiving comes to mind! Picnics, cookouts, parties—they all revolve around food.

The emotional pleasure we gain from eating, then, overrides the mental pain that we suffer because of the physical effects of overeating.

Many people have been able to make the rational, healthy decision to decrease the amount they eat—along with the types of food they eat—because they understand the physical effects. Others are forced into lifestyle changes because of massive pain due to heart attack, high blood pressure, or simply the physical discomfort of being overweight. The pain finally outweighed the pleasure (if you'll pardon the pun!)

Once again, we see the results of cause and effect on our lives.

If we associate pleasure with things that we know are bad for us, how did our judgment get so confused? The answer is in how our pain/pleasure associations were formed.

These associations were created in our minds as a result of programming.

Programming is simply the cumulative effect of influences throughout our lives, especially when we were young. Some programming is beneficial: you may have been raised to be thrifty with your money, or to enjoy eating vegetables more than junk food.

Other programming can be destructive. Bigotry, prejudice, hatred of those who are different—each results from the unreasonable bigotries, prejudices and hatreds of influences in our lives.

Even if we don't remember the particular occasions when we were taught these beliefs, they still have an effect on our judgments and opinions as adults. Our parents and family, our friends, acquaintances and other experiences all influence us. These forces shape our lives. They stay in our subconscious mind, guiding us without our even knowing it.

THE CONSCIOUS AND SUBCONSCIOUS MINDS

The *conscious* mind is the thinking mind. It's the part of our mind where we go to access information. The information we get there influences our thoughts, and our thoughts determine our feelings, and therefore, our actions. If you want to go on vacation, you decide where you want to go based on information you've gathered from various sources such as friends, television, movies, the internet, or some other place. You then figure out how to get there.

The conscious mind deals with ideas. When presented with an idea, the conscious mind can accept, reject, or neglect the idea. (It can also formulate an idea!) The decision on which of those courses to take depends on our viewpoint, established by the programming we have received (whether faulty or not) and our life experiences.

To render a decision, the conscious mind compares the idea to previous circumstances, so it has some sort of context. It acts as a filter in a way. If the idea is very similar to something that has occurred before, we are likely to judge the current idea based on the previous one. If the previous experience was pleasurable, we accept the idea. If it was painful, we reject the idea.

The conscious mind communicates and receives information from the world through the senses. If we want to communicate with the world, we use methods that stimulate the senses of another person. We speak so that someone else can hear what we say. We write so someone else can see our thoughts.

We ignore much of the information that is available to the conscious mind, otherwise we wouldn't be able to process all of it. In any given situation there are hundreds, if not thousands, of pieces of information coming at you through your senses. Paying attention to more than a few of these details would be so distracting that we wouldn't be able to function.

As children, we form beliefs that we carry with us the rest of our lives. Because our judgment is fallible, especially as children, many of our belief systems are built on erroneous judgments. Our conscious mind has developed, but with mistakes. However, with effort we can change our conscious mind and eliminate those misconceptions.

In contrast to the conscious mind, which deals with ideas upon which it can exert judgment, the *subconscious* mind works on a more subtle emotional level. The conscious mind expresses itself via the senses, whereas the subconscious uses feelings and emotions to communicate. This is the key to opening ourselves up to our potential. Unlike the conscious mind, the subconscious mind can not judge the information that it is presented with. Everything, whether real or imagined, is believed. It can't differentiate between the two.

I often compare the subconscious mind to a treasure chest. The subconscious mind is like a big chest hidden away in the attic. It can hold many valuable treasures—ideas about ourselves, or our self-image—that can further our progress. Or it can hold useless trinkets: useless ideas that disempower us and limit our performance. It's a useful process to review our performance and notice the trinkets that are hindering our progress and remove or replace them with more valuable possessions, ideas that can help us achieve our dreams and desires.

The subconscious mind accepts whatever idea it is given. True or not, an idea will plant itself in the subconscious and continue to exert its influence for as long as it can. When we are young, these ideas are implanted and become our belief systems. Those belief systems in turn cause us to make certain decisions at different times for the rest of our lives.

As you can imagine, the belief systems you hold exert tremendous power over the quality of your life. As children we didn't have the power or the resources to control the images that our subconscious mind took in. Every impression, every emotion, every trauma resulted in our forming a particular image and belief that we simply accepted as true. Even when the facts have changed, rendering the belief inaccurate, our subconscious still regards it as "true."

Another factor that gives the subconscious mind such power is that it is always working. On the one hand it regulates the body's response to sensations. A particular image may make us happy. The feel of a scratchy sweater irritates us. A smell may remind us of another situation, like the way apple pie baking in the oven reminds me of the time my Aunt Jean taught me how to make pastry. The sensations that come to us via our senses become filtered through emotional experience.

Besides the connection to the physical world, the subconscious mind also works at reinforcing the beliefs that it already holds. We may read a headline and automatically agree or disagree with it based on what we already believe. The human inclination is for us to seek out points of view that agree with our personal beliefs. The subconscious mind continually compares our experiences in the world with those beliefs, and evaluates them accordingly.

VALUES

Imagine you're at a funeral. The church is full of all the people in your life: family, friends, and coworkers, people who are in your church or in the organizations you belong to. You walk to the front of the church where the casket is on display, and you look inside. It's you in the casket. It's your own funeral.

Now imagine that a member of your family gets up to give the eulogy. What would you want that person to say about you as a son, daughter, brother, sister, mother or father?

Next a friend of yours does the same thing, and then someone from your church, or organizations that you may belong to. What would you want them to say?

The things that you want others to say about you when you are gone—when you no longer have any social interest in their opinions—is what you consider important.

One problem with this exercise is that most of us have given little consideration to what is most important to us. Sure, it's nice to have money, someone to love us, maybe good health—but beyond those few concepts, have you given any thought to your values? To the multitude of possibilities and their relative importance?

Take the three mentioned above: money, love and health. Which of these is most important to you? Money? Would you be happy if you were a millionaire and you only had a week to live? Probably not, right? So maybe good health is relatively more important than money?

The good thing about values is that they're not mutually exclusive. You can value wealth, love *and* health, if you like. Sometimes your values will bump against each other, and you will be forced to decide which is more important.

Other times your values will work together. "Hmmm, I value going to the beach, but I also value time with my kids." Boinng! "I know, I'll take the kids to the beach!"

The example above is a little silly, because most of us make those judgments all the time without going through the process step-by-step like that. It's a great illustration, though, that the process does take place, even if subconsciously.

Although that example is pretty simple, other times the decisions are not. If your cousin wants to borrow money, do you lend it to him? Depending on your values, that may or may not cause a conflict.

One value you might have is to cherish your family. If you had only that one value, your decision would be simple: lend him the money. Another value could be to handle your money responsibly. You might adhere to a budget so that you can keep your finances under control. Lending your cousin the money would disrupt your budget.

The trick in such a case is to see if, first, you can accommodate both values at the same time. For example, you might have money in savings that you could afford to lend him without jeopardizing your own finances. Or you may be able to help him in another way that solves his problem that doesn't involve money. For example, he might need the money for car repairs, and instead of lending him the money, you help him fix his car.

However, your value on money might be, "Don't lend money to family or friends." In a case like this, would you not help your cousin at all? Could you simply give him the money as a gift, one that doesn't involve his paying you back?

As you can see, your value systems are incredibly complex and interrelated. Sometimes they will work together smoothly, and other times they will conflict with each other so starkly that you will be forced to choose one over another.

At this point you may not even be aware of all the different values you already hold. No one else has lived your life. Siblings may share many of the same values, yet differ in key areas. Even twins, who share so much in their lives, and may have very similar values, may nevertheless place emphasis in different areas.

Try to think of occasions where your emotions were highly charged, and see if it was because one of your core values was being violated, or conversely, being observed. If instances come quickly and easily to you, then you're close to seeing the higher-priority values in your own life.

Start a values list, and begin prioritizing them. It can be difficult to create a values list out of thin air, so below is a list of possible values that you may hold. The list is not complete, of course, because the number of values both large and small that a person can hold is gigantic. The list is simply a starting place for you to be able to develop your own, more personal, list.

LIST OF PERSONAL VALUES

Accomplishment/Success – achieving conscious movement toward a chosen goal

Accountability – being liable for, or answering for, your actions

Accuracy – the quality of being correct or exact

Adventure – enjoying the exciting or unknown

All for one and one for all – a sense of loyalty toward, and responsibility for, the team or group from each of its members

Beauty – a love or admiration for physical attractiveness

Calm, peace – a state of mind without commotion or conflict

Challenge – a test or contest which requires effort and where success is not guaranteed

Change – an alteration from the present state; variety or novelty

Cleanliness – keeping things free of germs, dirt or grime

Collaboration – a commitment to working with others to complete a project or achieve a goal

Commitment – honouring a pledge or a promise; an obligation

Communication – exchanging information with another party

Community – giving importance to the group, culture or society to which one belongs

Competence – performing a task with skill and knowledge

Concern for others – placing importance on the wellbeing of parties other than yourself

Content over form – the fundamental idea is more important than its presentation; the steak, rather than the sizzle

Continuous improvement – the desire to move forward toward various goals

Cooperation – placing importance on working with others

Creativity – doing or thinking in an original way

Decisiveness – the quality of being final or decisively settled

Democracy – every member of a group has a say in the group's decisions

Discipline – strict adherence to rules or guidelines through training and control

Ease of use – readily utilized without the need for extra instructions; "user friendly"

Efficiency – accomplishment without unnecessary complications

Equality – all parties have the same value

Excellence – striving for the highest level of achievement

Fairness – each party has an equal chance

Faith – belief that is not based on proof; ***or*** belief in a higher being or in the doctrines or teaching of religion

Family – placing importance on those with whom you feel a strong kinship

Flair – doing things with a distinctive elegance or style

Freedom – existing without control from others; having a choice

Friendship – association with others with affection or personal regard

Hard work – exerting your utmost in energy and actions

Honesty – dealing with others in a forthright and true way

Honour – valuing honesty, fairness, or integrity in one's beliefs and actions

Independence – working without the interference or assistance of others

Knowledge – valuing education, ideas and learning

Leadership – the role of a person or persons directing the attitudes or actions of a group

Love/romance – a profoundly tender, passionate affection for another person

Maximum utilization – the use of all possible resources toward accomplishing a mission or achieving a goal

Merit – rewards based on actual achievement

Money/wealth – an abundance of financial resources

Openness – dealing with others without concealment of ideas or thought

Perfection – a state of completion without flaws or errors

Personal growth – the capacity of an individual to more fully reach his or her potential

Practicality/pragmatism – the realistic plausibility of an idea or action utilizing available resources

Preservation – to keep alive or in existence; make lasting

Problem solving – the willingness and capacity to resolve an issue

Progress – the belief in constant forward movement toward an ideal or a goal

Punctuality – the valuing of time and preciseness in appointments

Quality of work – providing the highest standard possible in products and tasks

Resourcefulness – the ability to creatively and effectively utilize available resources

Rule of law – the absolute authority of government rules and regulations

Self-reliance – the capacity to exist on one's own without the need to depend on others

Simplicity – freedom from complexity or intricacy; **or** an absence of luxury, pretentiousness or ornament

Speed – the need for things to move as rapidly as possible

Stability – continuance without change; permanence

Standardization – the quality of a process where one component can be substituted for another without loss of efficiency

Status – the position of an individual in relation to another or others

Strength – the quality of having power or being strong

Systemization – the process of arranging in or according to a comprehensive order or plan of procedure

Tolerance – understanding or forgiveness of different cultures, lifestyles or beliefs

Tradition – embracing beliefs or practices established in the past

Trust – placing faith in another person or situation

Unity – individuals of a group standing together for a common cause

Variety – enjoying a number of different types of things

Wisdom – knowing what is true or right, coupled with judgment as to action or insight

In the earlier example, the value of "family" might mean more to you than the value of "money." By thinking deeply about such questions, when the values do come into conflict, your decision making will be easier and more accurately reflect your priorities.

Besides the personal growth you will enjoy from the insights into your values, your value list can also have a more practical side. Major decisions can be made more quickly if you already know your values.

For example, if you are considering whether to take a new job in another city, if you value "adventure" more than "stability," then you have a good start on making a decision that is appropriate *for you.*

Perhaps you'd like to be "happy." Okay, that's sort of a given. But what do you really mean when you use the word *happy?* First of all, recognize that happiness and pleasure are highly individual. You are unique, and what makes someone else happy may not make you happy. Some people enjoy mowing the grass; others hate it.

What we're looking for here is a working definition that makes the whole process worthy. It has been said that a rising tide lifts all boats. If you are pursuing your own happiness, it could contribute to the wellbeing of others as well.

If you find that your happiness depends on the misfortune of others, or at their expense (a condition known as *schadenfreude,*) then you may want to reevaluate your values. This is not necessarily a moral judgment, but a useful one.

If you pursue a course of action that intentionally leads to another person's misfortune, there will eventually be consequences for you to suffer. Such consequences may be more severe than you imagine your actions call for. This will simply move you away from your goals.

The values list you create will likely be full of positive attributes. None of them depends on hurting anyone else. If you use those values, and have created others like them, then to be in line with your own values, your actions should follow the direction that your values point toward.

In psychology there is a condition known as *cognitive dissonance*. It's anxiety resulting from a conflict between one's beliefs and one's actions. If you have created a set of positive values, ones you want to be remembered for, then your actions should align with those values. Doing otherwise creates anxiety, and who can be happy living like that?

In time you will discover that your greatest pleasure and happiness will derive from working toward a worthy goal, one that contributes to your own wellbeing, the wellbeing of others, and to the benefit of society. Although you're only human and are prone to mistakes and backsliding, strive to live your life in accordance with your core values.

As you begin, take your time as you discover your Purpose. This is an important concept, and it's worth taking your time. Align your beliefs with your values. If they don't match up, consider whether you might need to alter some of your beliefs. Programming is potent, and unless you focus on improving the alignment between beliefs, values, and purpose, personal growth can be difficult.

Some people are fortunate enough to recognize their Purpose early on in life. Their passion is apparent from the start. David Castelino is one such person: he turned a childhood fascination with science into a true calling.

When he was only eleven years old, David received a science kit from his mother. Shortly afterward he began experimenting with solar energy. David is currently an engineering student at the University of Toronto, and his affinity for solar energy has continued unabated. In his second year of study, David was recognized for developing a cost-effective and less fragile solar tile.

David is also the recipient of the Duke of Edinburgh Gold Award, which recognizes youths between the ages of 18 and 24 for their accomplishments in several areas, including volunteerism, physical fitness, and developing social and practical skills. David has been named to Canada's Top 20 Under 20, a program that recognizes contribution from our youth.

Oh, and by the way, David also has a patent pending on a paint that can collect solar energy.

Your own recognition of your Purpose may not be as early or as dramatic as David's, but once you discover it, you will find that your life can be just as productive and fulfilling.

You have likely lived your entire life up to now without realizing the nature of your true Purpose. Now it's time to make changes so that you can live the rest of your life On Purpose.

MY PROMISE

I promise...

- to begin asking myself Big Questions,
- to reflect and remember moments of bliss in my life, thereby discovering my purpose,
- to think about decisions I've made and the programming that influenced them,
- to evaluate in what ways pain and pleasure motivate me,
- to think deeply about my values and prioritize them,
- to perform all of the above actions without judgment, and to be honest in my responses.

CHAPTER THREE

—Create Your Big Picture—

CHAPTER THREE
—*Create Your Big Picture*—

Sometimes high-minded thoughts can get in the way of achieving what we want to achieve. In our discussion of *purpose*, the emphasis was on the feeling of fulfillment, a state of timelessness and bliss that you have experienced at some point in your life. It was the moment that you were born for.

With that kind of buildup, who *wouldn't* be intimidated? You may be asking yourself, how is someone like little old me going to accomplish all that big stuff?

It's a good question, and you're not the first person to have doubts. As we go through the process of making your purpose a reality in your life, try to remember the deep feeling of fulfillment in those special moments. What you want to remind yourself of occasionally, is the emotion that is behind your efforts—the realization that you already have the resources to make those moments a reality. (Or else you wouldn't have the experience to remember in the first place, right?)

It makes sense to set up your world in such a way that you are in the position to enjoy that same feeling of recognition and fulfillment as much as possible. "Setting up your world" doesn't sound so intimidating, does it?

What you need now is a way to turn that purpose into reality. The next step in doing that is called your *vision*. I'm not talking about your eyesight here. I mean your ability to see things—places, situations, people—that don't yet exist. What I have in mind is more like the word "envision" —to picture something mentally, on the screen of your mind's eye.

Your vision will be the expression of your purpose. Whereas your purpose is essentially an emotion, your vision is that emotion made concrete. For example, maybe you realized that you feel most fulfilled when you are instructing others—sharing information or knowledge with them.

How would you set up your world where you can experience that feeling more often? You could use your *vision* to see yourself as a teacher at the front of a classroom, or as a tutor, giving one-on-one guidance to students. You might work as a trainer for a company. In any of these cases, you can see yourself actually performing these actions that evoke the emotions your purpose gives you.

Your vision will be the connector from the large picture—your purpose—to the actual execution of actions that make the purpose a reality. It's important to spend some time on this step. The better the quality of thinking at this point, the less chance you will have of missing your mark later.

I want you to remember one important thing as you consider creating your vision. In our culture we often get caught up identifying ourselves with what we do for a living. That's natural, given the number of hours we devote to our jobs. However, don't limit your vision to only your career. You are trying to find the best way to express your purpose in life, not necessarily the way to make the most money.

While we all want to work hard and become more successful, remember that you are not your job. Looking at your vision through only that prism limits the marvellous possibilities that life can provide. Don't restrict yourself unnecessarily. Sometimes a hobby becomes a passion and a purpose. Many people find their true calling as they pursue charitable or philanthropic endeavours. You might be one of these people.

CREATING A VISION

It's very difficult for some people to create a vision that they feel best expresses their purpose in life. In today's world – especially given the power of the internet – you have a multitude of choices for how you might pursue a particular dream. The trick is to use your imagination, let it run wild, and then sort through the possibilities that might occur to you as you seek to find the best, most elegant solution.

First of all, as we discussed earlier, *think of situations* where you felt the most fulfilled. Using that example, say you decide that you enjoy the feeling of sharing knowledge with others. Some of your options might include:

- Grade school or high school teacher
- College professor
- Tutor
- Technical support in a company, business or service
- Consultant
- Lecturer
- Public speaker
- Writer or author
- Community leader
- Coach (Don't restrict yourself to just athletics! There are all kinds of coaches!)
- Advisor
- Counselor

This list is by no means comprehensive. It's simply a start toward showing you the variety of ways that you can create a vision where you might share knowledge with others in a constructive way. It's the *situation* that matters, not the actual position.

One very effective tool that I like to use is a *vision board*. A vision board is a visual reminder of what it is you're striving for. The vision board can include photographs, drawings, charts—anything in which you can actually see what it is you are hoping to create.

For example, you may see part of your vision as including a vacation. You can get a poster board and put up photos of tropical islands (travel magazines are great for these!) or maybe just a tall cold drink with an umbrella in it. Use whatever it takes to excite your imagination so that your emotions are involved. Excitement about your vision is an absolute must!

The key is to create a visual reminder of what you want your life to be, have, or mean, and to include all areas where you want to make changes or improvements.

Another option is to *think of people* whom you admire and who are doing something similar to what you want to do. Do you feel most fulfilled when you are constructing business deals? Then Donald Trump, Warren Buffett or Ray Kroc (founder of McDonald's restaurants) might be examples you can emulate. Enjoy helping others? Think of Mother Teresa, Florence Nightingale, or Gandhi. What parts of their stories do you relate to most? Perhaps it's Mother Teresa's pursuit of helping those who don't have resources to help themselves. Maybe it's Florence Nightingale's ability to help soldiers (or others) who have suffered terrible trauma. You might identify with Gandhi's courage in standing up to authority to help those who are downtrodden.

In almost any vision that you might want to create, there is someone else who has done something similar. It may not be a perfect fit; times and conditions change, and are different for each of us. The inspiration of those who have accomplished great things in your area of interest is what you're looking for. Then you can adapt what they did to apply it to your own life.

Another way to create a vision is to *use active imagination* and think "What if?" For example, What if you could provide a good or service that was delivered directly to someone's home? Tom Monaghan did exactly that and created Domino's Pizza, one of the largest home-delivery pizza companies in the world.

When you use your imagination, don't limit yourself only to what you think is "possible." Given the technological and communication advances made in the last decade, accomplishing what was considered "impossible" just a few years ago is now easier than ever. Your potential market is the entire world.

At this point, let your imagination run wild. Your goal is to produce as many ideas as possible that could help you recreate the situations where you were touched by the feeling that you had found your true calling. There will be plenty of time later to sort through your ideas. As you are creating your vision, there are no limits to what you might do. The best way to come up with a *good* idea is to first come up with *a lot* of ideas.

ROLE MODELS

One of the points mentioned above was to think of people who are doing what you want to do. Such people are called *role models*. It's often useful to look around to find what kind of person is already living the type of life you want. Whom do you know who has already achieved the vision you are creating in your mind? If you're fortunate enough to have someone close to you that fits the description, you're in luck—you've found a role model.

Besides the example they provide, role models can show you exactly how they accomplished what they've accomplished. Financial expert Dave Ramsey says that he actively sought out millionaires when he was younger, inviting them to lunch and plying them with questions on how they earned their millions. His motto is, "Find people who did what you want to do, and do what they did."

Our world is filled with role models, but not always the kind that we want. Most of us are surrounded by people who have given up, who indulge momentary whims at the expense of larger goals, or whose lives are spent in indulging appetites rather than enriching their souls.

The challenge in using role models to help you create your vision is finding the right ones. Seeking out those whose paths are similar to the one you want to follow can be difficult, especially if your path differs from the paths chosen by those close to you.

There are different ways to find role models whose examples can help you reach your own goals.

Seek out those close to you. While I painted a rather bleak picture above, I didn't mean that there are *no* positive role models around you. If you want to be a good parent, look at your own parents. Find particular aspects of their parenting that worked, and duplicate them. Even if you're not perfect, with time and practice you will likely be able to duplicate their results.

Look around your neighborhood. There are those who may be great at listening, and you can learn from them. A restaurant's employees may provide fantastic service—seek out the owner or manager and see what they did to train those employees.

Is there someone in your town whose reputation for being honest and honorable is spotless? (We're all looking for a plumber or mechanic like that!) Find them and buy them lunch, and find out the actions they took and the sacrifices they made to achieve that kind of reputation. The point is to seek out people geographically close to you who have accomplished the things that you want to accomplish, and who have demonstrated the same values that you have and admire.

Role models from afar. For most of us, there are many, many role models who are not near enough to invite out to lunch. Their exploits and accomplishments are in tune with our own goals, but we are not able to have face to face communication with them.

Regardless of their sometimes high status, occasionally our heroes are close enough to contact. Bill Clinton was a teenager when he met his idol, John F. Kennedy. As a delegate to Boys Nation while in high school, he met President Kennedy in the White House Rose Garden. The encounter led Clinton to enter a life of public service.

Is your hero appearing anywhere nearby, perhaps to give a speech or some other presentation? Take the opportunity to attend, and if a question-and-answer session is available, take advantage of it. While they can't usually give lengthy answers to your questions, they will often give you an insight to their own success.

Sometimes it can be as simple as writing a letter. Many accomplished people are willing to answer a politely-written letter in which you explain your own goals and ask for advice.

If your hero doesn't respond to a letter, then try to read any articles or books he or she has written. Contemporary authors are often able to describe their story in more detail in a book. Biographies are also a great way to learn the story of your contemporary role model. Autobiographies are especially useful in that they are written in the person's own words. Biographies are also sometimes the only way to learn the secrets of success of people from the past. The life story of your hero can be both an inspiration and an instruction manual for anyone wishing to learn from them.

Sometimes you'll be fortunate enough to find a whole series of books by an author that explains his or her philosophy. One of my favourites is Napoleon Hill. Napoleon Hill's books have become legendary in providing the precise tools that he and many others have used and advocate in achieving success. Primary among the traits that Napoleon Hill recognized as required for success is desire. Among Hill's lessons is that all success begins with *desire*—the burning need to do, build, create, make, achieve. He said, "Desire is the starting point for all achievement—not a hope, not a wish, but a keen pulsating desire which transcends everything." From his tone, you can see that Hill differentiated between merely wanting something and having a burning desire for it. This is the type of lesson that ran like a thread throughout his works. His masterpiece was the book *Think and Grow Rich*. He wrote several books in his career, and all of them can be useful to you. Although Napoleon Hill passed away long ago, he has served as a mentor to hundreds of thousands of people. Because of his writings, recordings, and the personal training he provided, many people in his audience in turn became mentors themselves. Look for this kind of relationship, both near and distant, as you seek out people to learn from.

THE POWER OF YOUR IMAGINATION

You will often find that you're not able to find just the right role model for what you're trying to accomplish and the life you're trying to lead. What should you do when you've run out of other resources? Use your imagination.

The concept of using your imagination to achieve your goals may be foreign to you. You may in fact have been told not to spend so much time on your imagination.

The use of your imagination is a double-edged sword. If you spend too much time daydreaming aimlessly about what-if situations, then you are actually squandering time and improperly using one of your most powerful tools. When used properly, though, imagination provides you with the power to tap into energy and other resources you might not realize you already have.

What we're advocating here is the planned, structured use of *directed imagination.* The difference between directed imagination and simple daydreaming is that you're consciously deciding to use some of the same techniques you use when daydreaming to work toward a specific goal. You're daydreaming with a purpose. In this case, you're looking for a role model who has accomplished certain things, or achieved particular goals, or otherwise embodies the traits that you desire.

First you want to do proper research. If you've searched locally to find a role model, and you've read books and articles to find a person either living or dead who could serve as a role model, then you've already been exposed to some people who exhibit traits similar to the ones you want. You will be constructing a fully customized role model, taking a piece from one person, another piece from someone else, and so on until you've made a model close to what you want.

One way to idealize your role model is to think of the decisions and actions the person would take. Ask yourself, how would a person with the traits I'm looking for act? For example, someone who worked hard to earn a fortune, starting from nothing, might value earning more than someone who won the lottery.

Imagine your person looking over the phone bill to make sure he or she was charged correctly. Or you might imagine that same person tired, discouraged, wondering if the effort was worth it, and then going to the next sales call anyway.

Let's stop and play with that last image for a moment. What you could do is imagine the next sales call going well, and the feeling of triumph your role model would have by persevering. By using your imagination, you can actually feel the thrill of winning by overcoming obstacles.

Essentially you're asking yourself questions, and then answering them. Instead of a shallow, easy answer, though, you are using the power of your imagination to dig deeper, in coordination with your values, to find the *best* answer. While in many cases your first instinct is right, in this process you want to dig for more meaningful concepts than just your first flash of inspiration.

Another way you can approach the imagined role model is to make yourself the role model. Not the "you" that you are now, but the you that you would be if you had the particular traits you're looking for. The question to ask yourself is, "How would I act if I were that type of person?" Follow the same process described earlier, imagine not only the actual actions, but the emotions that would accompany the successful exhibition of a particular trait.

Make sure when you do this that your imagined role model is actively exerting influence on the situation in question. A passive scenario, where your role model is merely the recipient of good fortune—the "winning the lottery" fantasy, for example—falls back into mere daydreaming.

As you perform this exercise, you will become more adept at entering the special mindset necessary to creating a realistic and effective scenario. Push yourself to make your role models more insightful and creative, looking for ways to make your sessions of directed imagination more productive.

VISION AND GOALS

At some point, you have to take action to make your vision a reality. If you've decided you want to be a teacher, for example, you will likely need specific education and certification. The actions you take to create your vision are called *goals*. Goals are the specific steps, or milestones if you wish, that you take to achieve a larger objective. Any task, no matter how daunting, can be broken down into smaller, easier steps.

Of course, you can't simply spring into action and call it a "goal." We've all been guilty, at one point or another, of busily doing tasks without making any actual progress. Think how much more productive you would be if every action you took during the day was designed to move you forward toward a larger objective.

Goals are something to strive for, to move *toward*. Human beings are naturally hard-wired to accomplish things—to gather and eat food, to stay warm, to develop relationships. In other words, our natural instinct is to set goals that are *addition*, not *subtraction*.

When you consider your goals, remember that you are moving *toward* creating your vision. This creates a positive mindset, as you are moving forward rather than moving backward. The focus is on the ideal outcome, which is positive, rather than a sense of "loss," which would be negative. You are subconsciously resetting your internal "attitude barometer" so that you envision the new, ideal situation rather than the one you're leaving behind.

That's what setting goals is all about: making sure that your actions propel you toward creating your vision. With that in mind, it helps if your goals have particular characteristics. These characteristics have been shown over the years to produce the best results. Fortunately, they are easy to remember: simply think SMART.

The attributes that effective goals have are that they are Specific, Measurable, Achievable, Relevant and have a Timeframe.

Specific. Images have much more of an impact on us when they are specific. If I ask you to think of a car, you may think of some generic object. If I ask you to think of a red 1959 Ford Thunderbird with whitewall tires, you will likely have a much more vivid image in mind.

It's the same way with your goals. Perhaps your vision is to be a high school teacher. You realize that you need a college degree. That in itself is not a specific goal. A more specific goal would be: "I will earn a Master's degree in education from Harvard University." The more specific you can make your goal, the easier it is to know what action to take to make it a reality.

Measurable. Every January millions of people make New Year's Resolutions to lose weight. That's it: "to lose weight." This type of goal is so vague (and negative—it's subtracting rather than adding) that it defies any sort of definition of actually *achieving* it.

A quick side note about this very common goal: it's much better to determine what weight you want to be, and then focus all your weight-related goals toward reaching it. If you're 160 pounds, for example, and you believe 130 pounds would be a better weight, then focus your attention on becoming 130 pounds and releasing the excess energy.

It's always better if you can break down your goal into numbers or some other sort of segment that will help you: a) see progress toward your goal, and b) know when you've reached your goal.

For example, if you make a resolution to weigh 130 pounds (or move thirty pounds toward your ideal weight), you know exactly when you have reached that goal. It's measurable. For the example above, you may discover that you need thirty-six credit hours to achieve a Master's degree in education. As you attend classes, you can see exactly where you stand in relation to completing your degree.

Achievable. When you set a goal, you are devising a plan that lets you affect the outcome. Everything that you do is under your control and influence. You are able to achieve the goal through your own efforts. That's why some goals such as "win the lottery" are not really goals at all, but wishes.

One of the most rewarding realizations that you can come to in life is that success is available to you through your own efforts. Random events happen to all of us, of course, but even so, you can create your own future despite them. It takes energy, discipline and hard work, but if you make a plan and stick to it, you can achieve what you want.

That's why a goal being achievable is such a pertinent part of the process. You no longer base your happiness, success, or vision on random events or blind luck. Instead, you are marshalling your resources and guiding your efforts toward creating a fulfilling future.

Relevant. All kinds of goals exist. Some are small and some are large. Any of your endeavors, small or large, can benefit from directing your energies properly. However, when it comes to creating your vision, you want to focus the majority of your energy toward those actions that move you closer to that vision. The goal should be relevant, or important to moving you forward.

Does this mean that you should only set goals for creating your vision? Of course not. You have many facets to your personality and to your life, and you can set goals in any of these. Creating your vision may encompass a very specific part of your life. However, you don't want to spend the major part of your time and energy creating goals for relatively unimportant things, or mistaking a to-do list or list of errands for a set of goals.

Expend your energy on those things in your life which are most fulfilling and which give you the greatest sense of reward and accomplishment. You will find that such actions propel you toward reaching your goals and transforming your vision from imagination to reality.

Timeframe. Even the most well-designed goal will fail if there is never a deadline. Most people are able to procrastinate and put off doing a task or a chore as long as possible, unless they are given a timeframe in which to get it accomplished. I am always amazed by what I can accomplish just before I leave for vacation! (How much work seems to get done at the last minute?)

For example, if your goal is to save $1000, then you could save a dollar a month for a thousand months. You would certainly achieve your goal, but it would take over eighty years to do it—not particularly useful. However, if you said, "I will save $1000 within the next ninety days," you have created a timeframe in which to achieve your goal.

There is a saying that goes something like this, 'work expands to fill the time allotted for it'. Having a time limit on your goal creates a sense of urgency that makes achieving it a priority. Making the goals that help you create your vision a priority ensures that you don't get caught up in minor distractions. You stay focused. You keep your "eye on the prize."

One final point on your vision and goals. They are not written in stone. Give this process due and important consideration and thought. By doing this you will remain close to the core of your purpose. However, you are, after all, human, and you might see a better solution to your questions after you have devised your plan.

If you see a better path toward realizing your purpose in life, give it the same consideration and thought that you gave your initial plan. If you decide that it would work better to become a consultant rather than a school teacher, for example, adapt your plan.

Robert Burns wrote that "the best-laid plans of mice and men often go awry." (Actually, what he wrote was, "The best laid schemes o' Mice an' Men Gang aft agley." Nobody knows it like that, though!) Even when you have been diligent and thoughtful in the steps to create your vision, you will still need to remain flexible and adaptable. Doing that, you will still be able to make your vision a reality.

MY PROMISE

I promise...

- to create a visual reminder of what it is I am working toward,
- to look at my "vision board" daily to help me stay on track,
- to think "what if,"
- to look for examples of excellence I can emulate,
- to actively search for role models,
- to set effective goals, and
- to be flexible and adaptable in all of my plans.

CHAPTER FOUR

—Striving For Excellence—

CHAPTER FOUR

—*Striving For Excellence*—

From the lessons in the previous chapter, you have a roadmap of how you can move forward to create a type of life that you've only dreamed of. As with any map, however, it only *represents* what you need to do to create that life. You still have the actual doing ahead of you.

To help accomplish what you want to do—in real life, not on paper—certain traits, characteristics and habits will certainly help. Ben Franklin's adage, "Early to bed, early to rise, makes a man healthy, wealthy and wise," describes such traits. Make no mistake: making sure you're following a plan and working hard to achieve it will put you well on the way to achieving your goals.

However, just staying busy, even with a plan, can still leave you frustrated. You have to put your mind in the right place to be most effective. You have to believe with all your being that you are capable of the greatness that you hold inside you. That greatness is called *potential*.

Most of us have heard the word potential used before, but it may have always seemed abstract and not really anything that was applicable to your own life. After all, you're just an ordinary person, right? The prospect of living an *extraordinary* life, achieving *great* things, might have actually scared you.

In her book *A Return to Love*, Marianne Williamson wrote: "Our deepest fear is not that we are inadequate. Our deepest fear is that we are powerful beyond measure." The unknown can be frightening, and to be able to achieve greatness in your life—well, that's simply too much unknown all in one bite!

The truth of the matter, however, is that you have locked inside you the potential to accomplish, do, and be more than you think is possible. If you are able to harness all of your resources and get out of your own way, you can create a future for yourself that is more fantastic than you've ever imagined.

The future, after all, is simply a reality that doesn't exist yet. Everything we do moves us toward that reality. The things you do now affect what that future will be. If you do the right things, then that future can be whatever you want it to be. *Potential*—that word you may have heard or even used yourself, without really thinking about the magnitude of possibilities—is the maximum wonderfulness that your own future might hold.

Potential is what would happen if you took all of your talents, skills, and actions, and put them into the right circumstances. It's like planting a seed under the ideal conditions and watching it grow to great heights and beauty. You have to know what you're doing, do the right things, and nurture it.

The funny thing is that an individual's potential is a moving target. As you move toward your potential, based on where you are now, you increase your knowledge, talents, skills and other attributes. You "grow" into the goal. Something that might have seemed to be too big for you before, now seems to fit. Simply by working toward one goal, you become capable of achieving another, higher goal.

If we take a moment to look at it, we could call achieving our potential the same thing as achieving perfection. But in the process of achieving your potential, you improve yourself, and therefore increase your potential. By this standard, it is impossible to achieve your full potential, just as it is impossible to achieve perfection. However, what you have managed to do along the way is to achieve *excellence*.

EXCELLENCE AS A WAY OF LIFE

"Excellence" is one of those concepts that we all pretty much recognize, but we aren't often asked to put into words. Tom Peters authored a great book, *In Search of Excellence*, in which he attempted to define excellence in companies. He listed attributes such as paying attention to customers, going the extra mile to provide service, and so on.

Most people will understand when you say that excellence is something that is unusually high-quality. It's more than just "good," because many things can be described that way: a good cook, a good worker, etc. It's a compliment, but relatively common. The key is that we're talking about something that is *unusually* good, the type of work you don't see every day.

In its unusualness, excellence exceeds the normal everyday standards, which often include the simply "good." An excellent result, whether in throwing a baseball, making sales, or baking a cake, calls attention to itself because it stands out from the rest of the bunch.

The ancient Greeks had a word that is often translated as excellence: *arete*. It is an interesting concept because beyond recognizing something as high-quality, *arete* also indicates the fulfillment of purpose or function. In other words, as you more closely approach fulfilling your purpose in life, the more excellence you create as a standard of what you do. Those ancient Greeks knew something!

When you talk about *excellence*, you may have someone in your life ask, "Why bother? Good is good enough." For many people who are afraid of change, or who are nervous about what they might actually be capable of, that philosophy is what gets them through the day. So how do you answer a question like that? What *are* the benefits of striving for excellence?

First, of course, is higher-quality work. It's the manufacturer whose products are consistently more precise and closer to specifications. It's the computer programmer whose programs seem to work more smoothly, with fewer bugs and taking up fewer resources. It's the clerk in the clothing store whose customers leave with a better fit and who feel as though they've received personalized service.

See how excellence can be pursued in any endeavor you try? Everyone appreciates excellence in craftsmanship or service, regardless of how large or small it may seem to others. Whether in finding the perfect pen, having our cell phone problems resolved quickly with a single call to customer service, or driving a car that runs like a top, we all want superior quality— *unusual* quality—in the items and services we use every day.

Another benefit is something that, once again, the Greeks understood. They called it *eudemonia*. (Yes, I know it sounds like some sort of disease!) The concept can be described as the highest good that humans can achieve, recognizing and fulfilling one's purpose, and experiencing the satisfaction and fulfillment of living a life well-lived. It's the joy of a job well done. Those who settle for "good enough" in their lives miss out on this pleasure.

Pursuing excellence is not simply a matter of enjoying yourself, though. The benefits extend beyond the individual and affect others as well. The people who depend on your product or service get a higher quality product as well. *They* are the ones who get to enjoy that perfect writing instrument, or the precisely manufactured, maintained, or repaired automobile. Through your efforts you bring joy to the world around you.

What's more, your pursuit of excellence can serve as an example to others. Have you ever been so inspired by someone whose high quality craftsmanship or service—whose *excellence*—was so great that you wanted to do better work too? Such people demonstrate the concepts of *arete* and *eudemonia*, probably without knowing those words. By simply showing that such excellence exists, they can open other people's eyes to the possibility of being excellent.

Many of us have been inspired by a teacher or a coach who worked hard to do the best job possible, and who brought out the best in us. Think of the impact such parents could have on their children! Their legacy of excellence is passed on to future generations.

So how does a person go about beginning their path toward excellence? First of all, they have to know that excellence exists, and decide that they will no longer settle for "good enough." After that it takes practice—lots of practice.

You may have heard the old saying, "Practice makes perfect." What I think it really means is that you have to practice excellence in order to achieve excellence. A rule of thumb is that it takes 10,000 hours of practice to master a skill, art, or craft. That's twenty hours a week for ten years!

That sounds intimidating, and it can be if you only look at the end product. What happens, though, is that as you practice producing and providing higher quality, your work becomes *more excellent*. Very few things in life are mastered on the first try, but the more you strive for improvement, the better you become. Incrementally, you increase the "excellence level" in your life.

What this means is that excellence takes time. Fortunately for most of us, we don't have to become "masters" of anything in order to do things better. We gradually increase the quality of whatever it is, until that becomes the standard for us, and one day we find that what we do is unnaturally good: excellent.

Excellence becomes a habit. We all have habits for different things in our lives. Habits are the actions that we do unconsciously, with little thoughtful effort. You can consciously *develop* the habit of excellence. In doing so, you will begin to find that you are able to achieve better results simply as a matter of course, because of the force of habit.

Striving for excellence, as with most good things in life, is not always easy. We all have human weaknesses, and they may occasionally try to assert themselves and resist the changes we want to implement. Our minds wander, we feel lazy or lethargic, or our attention span may be a little shorter than we like. In such cases we simply have to shake ourselves out of it and press on.

Sometimes we may have old habits that are counter to the pursuit of excellence. Pay attention to such habits and see how they work against you. Remember, we're trying to replace such habits with the habit of excellence. Don't beat yourself up if you catch an old habit hampering your efforts. Just pretend that it's an old acquaintance that you don't care to see any more, and work on reinforcing the new habit. Habit is a powerful force, so put it to work for you.

When we first try to make changes, simple inertia can make change hard. A body at rest tends to remain at rest, after all, so you may have to exert a lot of effort and energy at the beginning to get started. Remember your purpose, and the power of habit, and you will find that implementing your plan for excellence becomes easier.

Finally, you will sometimes find that the people around you are unsettled by your focus on excellence. It's sad to say, but most people in life become content with the way things are, and your setting a higher standard threatens their outlook. Keep in mind that you are working on yourself, not on them, and that others will benefit from your excellence.

With all this talk of achieving the *benefits* of excellence, some people might ask, is there a downside? There's always the chance that as you work to produce higher quality results, that others will come to expect a high standard from you. That's a wonderful reputation to have. When others know that you do excellent work, they will be attracted to dealing with you.

If being held to a higher standard scares you, remember that achieving excellence becomes easier as you continue. With the same, or in some cases, less, effort, your ability to produce *unusually good* work will grow. The more you practice excellence, the easier it becomes.

Think of excellence in your life not as a goal, but as a process. When you consistently strive for continuing improvement, excellence becomes a byproduct of your work. Remember what the ancient Greeks knew – the biggest payoff is that you are moving toward fulfilling your potential.

Once you realize that achieving your full potential is impossible, but that striving for it leads to extraordinary results, you begin to really believe in what you have inside you. Your potential is more than your current situation—it's what you can *do* when you strive to *be* as great as you can *be*.

We're talking about real life here, not something abstract. Of course there will be hard work, disappointments, changing situations and all the other challenges that life presents. Always keep in mind, though, that within you lies the seed of greatness. Nurture it properly, and you can overcome whatever life throws at you.

By now you may have started to see a theme. You are an individual with your own purpose in life. You have a unique vision of how to create your own particular life. Within you lie great resources that you were either born with, or which you acquired through your unique life experiences.

You are the best *you* in the world.

You have unique gifts and strengths that enable you to do things that most other people can't do. Those gifts and strengths are what make you an individual, unique from everyone else. Those attributes are part of what you can use to reach your potential.

Think about it. Have you ever known a salesperson who is great at overcoming objections? Have you ever known a cook who is great at throwing dinner parties? Have you ever known a manager who can come up with imaginative solutions to problems? All of these people have unique gifts that make them good at what they do.

These are examples of people whose activities emphasize their strengths. The manager might be a great cook, but that's not what he uses on the job. The cook might be great at overcoming objections, but that's not a very useful skill at a dinner party.

As you work at achieving your goals, find ways to use your own unique gifts and strengths. Put yourself in situations where you can shine, where you are able to do not just successful work, but *extraordinary* work. When you are exceptional at a certain thing, working with that strength separates you from the crowd.

This advice is not only for individuals. Stories of companies who excel at a single thing are commonplace. You think of their name, and you think of a single product. Harley-Davidson makes great motorcycles. Mercedes makes great cars. Each of these companies became exceptional at one thing. For both people and companies, *differentiation*—showcasing your unique attributes—separates you from others.

Whether it's in the work you do or the product you offer, you can emphasize your strength in what you choose to do or offer. You fly higher, faster, and farther when you acknowledge and utilize the gifts you have.

What if you're not sure what your strength is? (Sometimes we're simply *too great* at *everything*, aren't we?) If you haven't found your unique gift yet, do some research—you'll find an answer soon enough.

First think back on your own experiences. You did this before when finding your purpose, and this is similar. Has there ever been a time when you achieved results far better than anyone else? Or achieved results far better than you expected? Are certain things easier for you than they seem to be for other people?

One great clue of your unique strength is when you do something really well, but can't explain exactly how you do it. (If you ever knew the right answer on a math quiz in school, but couldn't "show your work," then you know what I'm talking about.) Gifts often have a way of making themselves known without actually announcing their arrival.

Another way to find your strength is simply to ask people around you. Those who *know* you best are in a perfect position to see you *at* your best. They'll remember occasions when you impressed them—probably times you never gave a thought to. Talk to more than one person to get the most accurate picture. What impresses one person may or may not impress another.

Once you've asked around, see if there is a common thread to all of the answers. Does one person say you're good at math, while another likes how you come up with creative solutions to problems? That may mean that you are an excellent analytical thinker. One friend likes your clothes, while another says your home always looks stylish? You may have a sense of style, or design, or an eye for how things will look. Think the answers over.

Another way is to think about what you have learned or accomplished recently. Have you added a key element that makes you capable of something special? Studying building materials, when combined with your eye for design, may be the last block you need to become a great architect.

Remember, as you work to improve yourself, you will often acquire complete *sets* of skills that make you able to do something completely outside of what you have considered in the past. Whenever you learn something new, see if you can combine with your existing skills to do something special.

Whenever we discuss our strengths, it's natural to think about our weaknesses. Some people ask, "Shouldn't I work on my weaknesses?" The answer is complicated, but I believe the answer is, "Yes, but don't spend too much time on them." Let me explain why.

Weaknesses will be a source of frustration and anxiety for you. Shoring up your weaknesses may make you more "well rounded" in a particular area, but memorable achievement is created when you use your strengths.

If a particular feature, habit or trait is absolutely crippling your efforts to succeed, you of course want to eliminate or lessen the effect of that weakness.

Earlier in the chapter, I spoke of traits, or attributes, that prove useful to anyone who is serious about fulfilling his or her potential. Two particular traits stand out in my mind: *focus* and *persistence*. Acquire and use these traits, and you will be well on the way to achieving any goals you set for yourself.

FOCUS

Remember a while back when I mentioned that reaching your potential depends, among other things, on taking the right actions? The question you may have—*what are the right actions?* —is something worth considering.

You may be good at many things, but do one particular thing extraordinarily well. To achieve the best results, doesn't it make sense to do that one particular thing more often? At some point, however, you run into the constraints of time. Each of us only has twenty-four hours in a day. What separates the great from the good, however, is what you get done within that time.

What that means is that you will need to *focus* your activities: exclude some things while doing other things more.

Focus, like *potential*, is probably a word that you have heard used very often, but without really thinking about the impact that it can have on your life. A piece of wisdom that I have learned is this: *when you can focus on the most important things, you are able to achieve more.*

Focus means narrowing your attention, your resources and your actions. As mentioned above, it's a process of excluding less important items on your to-do list in favor of other, more important things.

When you were a child, you may have spent time learning how to use a magnifying glass. If you're like most children—or at least like I was—you may have learned to use the glass to focus the sun's energy to set a piece of paper on fire. The sun has a huge amount of energy—both light and heat—that keeps us warm and out of the dark. When you choose to focus that energy, you are able to create such intense heat that it can cause fire.

In the same way, you have an enormous amount of energy—your potential—inside you. While dissipating that energy can make your life comfortable, *focusing* the energy can produce intense results. The greater your focus, the greater the effectiveness you will achieve.

In other words, your actions in life, and the actions you choose to take as you work toward your goals, can have either more or less effectiveness. The more effective you are, the more efficiently you can reach your goals.

Sales people and others involved in marketing understand the strength of focus. Because it's very difficult, if not impossible, to provide *everything* that someone might want or need, the so called "shotgun" approach is usually not the best bet. Marketing experts focus their attention on a particular group of customers that are either most appropriate for, or the biggest users of, their product.

Think about the advertising for modern electronic gadgets. Ads and commercials usually feature young people enjoying the particular product. Electronics manufacturers know that the majority of their customers are young, and design everything with that market in mind.

For example, cell phones used to be just for making calls. Now they are used as video cameras and personal radio stations. The customers can store hundreds if not thousands of songs – a feature that appeals to young people who don't want to be tied to a radio.

Other industries recognize the wisdom of niche marketing. The real estate salesperson who tries to sell both commercial and residential properties quickly runs into the fact that those two markets are decidedly different. Families looking to buy a home constitute a different market from individuals looking to invest in office buildings.

In business, as in your personal life, focusing your efforts on a very specific goal makes you much more productive.

I really can't emphasize the importance of focus enough. Although you may have unlimited potential, the amount of resources you have at any given moment—your attention, your time, your money—may be limited. You don't want to unnecessarily squander those resources. Using them in the most effective way produces the best results.

One word about *effectiveness*. I use the word to refer to the quality of your life, and the impact a decision or action has on achieving your goals. Your goal may be to buy a cup of coffee for a dollar. If you have only seventy-five cents, you can use your time to bemoan your bad luck (ineffective) or you can earn a quarter (effective) and buy the coffee. How you spend your time determines when you reach your goals.

Another way to think about focus is to consider building a house. If you have two boards that you want to connect, you use a hammer and a nail. You can hammer on the boards all day long, and you'll never get the house built. Hit the nail, though, and eventually you have a home. It's only by focusing the hammer's energy that the nail ever does its job.

In the same way, you can consider both the actions that you take to achieve your goals, and the goals themselves. Goal setting is a terrific tool to use in every aspect of your life. Regardless of how large or small the objective, breaking it down into achievable steps makes it easier to achieve.

When you think of your purpose and vision in life, certain goals have more impact than others. While it's worthy to have a number of goals for different aspects of your life, make sure that you are devoting the majority of your resources to those goals that move you closer to making your vision a reality. The more important the goal, the greater the resources it should receive.

If you try to achieve many goals at the same time, you won't achieve any of them. You can accomplish whatever you want, of course, but at any given time you should be working on the most important things first.

Charles Schwab, the founder of Bethlehem Steel, once hired a consultant to help his executives use their time better. However, he didn't have much time for extended studies, research, or seminars. He needed something quickly.

The consultant handed Schwab a blank piece of paper. "List what you need to do each day on this paper, in order of importance. Start with the most important item first, and don't do anything else until it's completed. Then move to the next most important thing, and don't do anything else until that is completed. Each day do the same thing."

Schwab shrugged at such a simple idea. "How much do I owe you?"

The consultant said, "Try it for a month, then pay me what you think it's worth."

At the end of the month, Schwab sent the consultant a check for $25,000. Schwab had found that focusing his energies on the most important items ensured that they got done. Anything that he didn't get done was, by definition, less important. Charles Schwab learned the importance of focus.

Decide what is most important in helping you make your vision a reality. Spend your time on those items, and you will be on your way to realizing the purpose that you are made for.

When you realize your unique strength, and structure your world so that you showcase it, then you start to specialize. *Specialization* is one of the key ingredients in becoming successful in today's world. If you're in real estate sales, you may specialize in commercial properties. If you are a chef, you may specialize in French cuisine. Whatever you decide to specialize in, it will establish you as an authority in that field.

Think about Olympic athletes. The best sprinters specialize in running events; you don't see any world-class sprinters also throwing the discus. They spend all of their time training intensely for a few events where their own unique gifts are put to best use. When they win the gold medal, no one complains that the athletes can't throw heavy objects. They are lauded for their success in that one event, and become part of history because of it.

PERSISTENCE

Persistence is the ability to keep moving toward your goals, despite hardship, setbacks, and adversity. When the force of your will is so strong that you simply refuse to be defeated, it is amazing what you can accomplish.

Nowhere has this been better illustrated than by the actor Christopher Reeve. Paralyzed in a horse riding accident, Reeve had trouble breathing and minimal movement of his head. Nonetheless, he kept an upbeat attitude and continued to work professionally in different capacities in show business. Moreover, he provided a tremendous example for others who have faced challenges.

Reeve once said, "So many of our dreams at first seem impossible, then they seem improbable, and then when we summon the will, they soon become inevitable."

Salespeople face adversity every day as part of their profession. They hear the word "no" many times before they hear a "yes." Successful salespeople learn the art of persistence simply through sheer repetition and brute force. They develop the strength of character that keeps them optimistic and upbeat—characteristics that are essential for anyone wanting to succeed in the profession.

Does this mean that salespeople (as a group) are "better" than the rest of the population? Of course not. What it means is that they have had to develop a success trait as part of their job. They may have sales goals, or income goals, or some other driving force that they keep in mind as they conduct their business. They can't afford to focus—there's that word again—on how many "nos" they may hear; they have to concentrate on the "yesses" that will help them achieve their goal.

That same trait can help anyone achieve their dreams. They focus on the payoff when they succeed, working through the obstacles that may present themselves along the way. That's how you develop persistence, by keeping your eye on the prize.

Let me refer back to the great Napoleon Hill. He once said *"There may be no heroic connotation to the word 'persistence,' but the quality is to a person's character what carbon is to steel."*

It's recognizing the great potential that you have within you, focusing your energies and resources on those items that help you reach that potential, and practicing persistence as you pursue your potential, that will help you create an excellent life. Living an excellent life is a fantastic "gold medal" to shoot for.

MY PROMISE

I promise...

- To recognize that I have unique gifts and strengths,
- To focus my actions on those unique strengths,
- To develop the traits and habits that help me realize my potential,
- To aim for excellence rather than perfection,
- to practice persistence in all I do,
- to strive for excellence in myself, and
- to acknowledge and learn from excellence in others.

CHAPTER FIVE
—An Inward Journey—

CHAPTER FIVE

—*An Inward Journey*—

It is one of the more interesting paradoxes in life that in order for you to believe in yourself fully, you have to believe in something greater than yourself. For some people, the belief lies in religion. For others, it's a philosophy that the universe is full of mysteries that we don't yet understand. Whether you call it fate, karma, or the "cosmic wheel," your potential is based on the idea that there is some order to the universe.

What I'm talking about here is the realization that, as Shakespeare wrote in *Hamlet*, "there are more things in heaven and earth, Horatio, than are dreamt of in your philosophy." It's simply not humanly possible for us to understand everything that the universe contains.

I certainly don't propose to give you such answers. What I can do, however, is help you tap into some of the mysteries that exist so you can create a life that is more full, more rewarding, and more worthwhile.

We've all heard the phrase "what goes around comes around." That's a simple statement that acknowledges the fact that how we treat others is usually reflected back on us at some point. Some people call it the "Universal Law of Reciprocity". What we give is what we receive.

This is just one instance of our belief in, and the inevitability of, universal mysteries. Just as we can't fight the law of gravity, there are certain laws that it benefits us to work with, not against. Treating other people with respect and a spirit of generosity is one way we work with the Universal Law of Reciprocity.

Regardless of what you believe in, it's important to your emotional and spiritual health that you believe in *something*. Without a foundation of belief, the world is simply too hard, too difficult, for most of us to contend with.

Let me break this down to something that you can apply to your own life. All of us have a core set of beliefs. Certain things feel right, and other things feel wrong. Our concepts of "right" and "wrong" may be based on religious beliefs, on our philosophy of life, or simply that old "cosmic wheel." Regardless of how you arrived at your beliefs, it harms you when you go against them.

Such concepts or beliefs are called *values*. When your actions align with your values, it's called *congruency*. Think of the times that you did "the right thing" even though it was painful or simply uncomfortable. You knew that ultimately it was the right thing to do. When you consistently do the right thing—according to your own values—you achieve an inner peace that lets you achieve a certain amount of mental relaxation and emotional calm.

This might be something as simple as doing without a luxury purchase so that you can pay your bills, or put the money to better use. You experience the discomfort, the disappointment of doing without something that you really, really want, so that you accomplish another, more important, goal.

When you make this kind of a choice, you are able to relax. The temporary discomfort dissipates, but the satisfaction of knowing that you made the right choice stays with you forever. What's more, when you consistently make such choices, it becomes easier to do the right thing in the future. This is what I mean when I talk about living a congruent life.

The process of knowing, understanding, and evaluating your values is a step toward greater self awareness. The ancient Greeks had a saying: "Know thyself." As I mentioned earlier, we sometimes have to deal with puzzling situations. Being aware of your own personality and priorities—knowing yourself—sets you on the road to being able to understand other people better. By understanding and helping other people, you become in tune with the laws that already exist in the universe.

There is a great connectivity to the world that we can't understand. In all your actions and dealings with others, you set in motion a great series of events that will eventually have an impact on your own life. Sometimes the connection between these events is easy to see, and other times impossible. That connection exists, however, and in everything you do, you should keep it in mind.

I believe that we are, as a philosopher once stated, "spiritual beings having a physical experience." Our thoughts are spiritual in nature. We have the ability to originate ideas, and so we are creative beings. We experience our creativity whenever we use our imagination. We also have the ability to create our imaginings on the physical plane. This ability is the product of acquiring knowledge and ingenuity during our lifetime. We can even collaborate with others to use their expertise in creating what we have imagined.

ENERGY

I believe that we are a mass of energy, vibrating at magnificent speed. What is thought, if not energy? The universe is full of the essence of thought. Imagination, creativity, and visualization are all forms of energy that exist in the human mind. Science teaches us that energy cannot be created or destroyed, but can only change in form. It always was, and always will be. Only its expression changes.

Consider water. At a very low temperature—32 degrees Fahrenheit, 0 degrees Celsius—it changes into ice. Warm that piece of solid ice up a bit, and it becomes liquid, or water. Heat it up even more, and it begins to boil. Soon you have steam, a gas. If you do this in an enclosed area, the steam will collect on surfaces as condensation, and begin the cycle all over again.

The argument for there being something greater than ourselves is very convincing. If we know that we are a mass of energy, with incredible gifts of intellect, isn't it reasonable to conclude that there is much more to us than what we can physically perceive? Just as water has the ability to change its expression, isn't it reasonable to conclude that we can as well?

We see some indications of our ability to tap into our energies when we express certain virtues, such as Service, Contribution, Faith and Gratitude. These attributes have always been tied to success. Napoleon Hill studied five hundred of the most influential and wealthy men over a twenty-five year period, and devoted an entire chapter of his book, *Think and Grow Rich,* to their commitment to these virtues.

Whatever your beliefs about religion and spirituality, developing a strong faith in yourself, along with a belief that you can achieve whatever you desire—combined with expressing gratitude for the good that is coming your way—is guaranteed to speed up its delivery. You will be walking in confidence.

AUTHENTICITY

When we put this all together, we have described a way of life that is both spiritual and practical. It's spiritual in the sense that we can't really understand or explain everything, and it's practical in the sense that the choices we make absolutely have an impact on our own quality of life.

Despite the waves of different problems, obstacles, and hurdles that you face, the degree to which you stick to your own values is the degree of *authenticity* that you exhibit. You stay true to yourself, to your own personality and beliefs, regardless of the temptations to act otherwise.

Authenticity shines in everything you do and every choice you make. It can't be faked, at least not for long. Haven't you ever dealt with someone and come to realize that everything they do is an essential part of their personality? Even when you can't predict exactly what they'll do in a situation, you can predict the *kind* of thing they'll do.

Of all the positive attributes that a person can possess, authenticity is near the top of the list. People close to you will admire you for it, and even people who may not like you (and we hope that's a short list, but you can't please everyone) will have respect for you.

As you consider personal spirituality, here are some points to ask yourself:

- What are my spiritual beliefs?
- How do I express my spirituality?
- Do I conduct myself in my day to day business with authenticity?
- How can I give to my community?
- What am I grateful for?

GLOBAL SPIRITUALITY

We live in a world which has plenty of problems. There is great tension as people rebel against their living conditions, their governments, or any number of other issues. More and more, hope seems to be fruitless, as the world seems to spin faster and faster.

Many of these unhappy people live without a sense of spiritual self. If they think of themselves as anything, it's that their lives are reduced to nothing more than a "carbon-based life form." They are left without an individual sense of spiritual worth. Where a sense of the spiritual is missing, often the baser instincts invade.

Imagine the energy I mentioned earlier, balled up inside each one of us, making creative thought and intelligence possible. What we can imagine, we can make real. Think of the possibilities if the entire world were able to tap into its spiritual side and make the dreams and aspirations of people everywhere come true.

The talk of a spiritual side is very personal. As with many things, however, what affects one of us affects all of us. Encourage the spiritual side in yourself and in those around you. I'm not talking about proselytizing or discussing religion in inappropriate situations. What I mean is serving as an example of the power of spirituality, and developing and commending it in others.

What I've described in this chapter is one of the foundations of the process of living a fulfilling life. Life is not just an aimless, empty pursuit. You already possess guidelines for your life, rules to live by. Spend time developing your spirituality and self awareness, and all other aspects of your journey to success will become much simpler and rewarding.

MY PROMISE

I promise...

- To live authentically
- To recognize the Law of Reciprocity
- To be a purveyor of good will and encouragement
- To recognize, commend and develop spirituality in others

CHAPTER SIX
—Playing Well With Others—

CHAPTER SIX

—*Playing Well With Others*—

The English poet and philosopher John Donne once famously wrote, "No man is an island, entire unto itself." How we interact with another person connects and ripples across multiple lives. Every conversation and every action affects that one person and that person's impression of us. That person interacts with other people in a way that reflects that impression.

What are the lessons that we have discussed so far? Mainly that you approach the different areas of your life with the "big picture" in mind. You think about your purpose, your vision and your mission. In every situation you try to think of ways that you can grow as a human being.

If we apply the lessons to our relationships, imagine how much deeper and more fulfilling each of them can be. Think of the things that have been done when people cooperated and worked together to achieve a larger goal. When people work together toward a common goal, they are capable of doing much more than if each of them worked alone.

One of the most important lessons my parents always reminded me of was the golden rule: treat others the way you would want to be treated. It applied to everyone, from complete strangers to my sister!

What are relationships? They are the interactions that we have with every other person. **You have relationships with:**

- family
- friends

- acquaintances
- coworkers
- customers
- strangers

When it comes to relationships, the first thing most people think of is their family. Some families enjoy close, supportive relationships with their parents, their brothers and sisters, their children, and their extended family, such as aunts, uncles, cousins, and grandparents. They have learned early in life the benefit of these relationships, as well as how to develop the skills necessary to be part of such relationships.

Others, for various reasons, are not fortunate enough to have such happy relationships. Broken families, single-parent (or even no-parent) families, dysfunctional families—these have all become common in today's harsh society. Even when a family is intact, there can be distance and coolness between family members that prevent the development of close bonds.

Then there are the friends that most people have. You likely have some very close friendships with people who you can count on to "cover your back," while other friendships have a bit more distance between you. The measurement of friendships is along a spectrum, from good friends, to some who might be better described as "friendly acquaintances."

Most of us have a large network of acquaintances, individuals with whom we come in contact regularly, but who are not close enough to be considered friends. The person who cuts your hair or checks your groceries at the supermarket, your mailman, your dry cleaner—you depend on all of these people for their contributions to your wellbeing. You're not close enough to share all the details of your life story with them, but you rub up against them often enough so that your interactions with them are significant.

Your coworkers may fit into both categories. Some of the people with whom you work may be your friends, while others are little more than acquaintances. (In large companies, some coworkers are complete strangers!) Coworkers are significant in that we often spend more time with them than we do with our own families. Regardless of our profession, most of us try to project a professional image when dealing with coworkers. With a few we share parts of our lives, and the information we share may or may not complement the image we present to the rest of the company.

As a member of a business, either as employer or employee, you likely have some dealings with customers, even if only occasionally. These interactions reflect not only on you personally, but also on your business. If you are warm, caring, and helpful with a customer, he or she will likely have the same impression of your company.

When you are in sales, your job requires you to have extensive interactions with customers. Every professional salesperson knows that the relationship he has with his customers can make or break his paycheck. An effective salesperson can't afford to be haphazard in his relationships with customers. Those interactions are the very essence of the salesperson's job.

Finally, the interactions we have with strangers often affect us. If you are driving to work and another car cuts you off, do you respond calmly or do you go directly to road rage? Does that anger carry over into your workplace? Such casual, one-time interactions with strangers can cause us to do or say things that we normally would avoid.

On the other hand, have you ever been touched emotionally when a stranger opened a door for you, or helped you pick up items you dropped? The entire plot of the movie "Pay It Forward" is based on strangers helping one another, without thought of reward. All they ask of the person they help is to "pay it forward."

These interactions with others, whether with family, friends, or strangers, are what establish the value of your lifetime. If relationships and interacting with other people are of low value to you, and you avoid them your whole life, then your life will be like a stone thrown into a pond: the ripples will last for just a few minutes, after which it will be as though you were never there.

On the other hand, if you value other people and treat them with respect and honesty, then your life will be well spent. Not only the quality of your time on earth, but also the example and lessons you provide during your lifetime will positively affect hundreds, if not thousands, of people.

IMPROVING YOUR RELATIONSHIPS

In his book, *The 7 Habits of Highly Effective People*, Stephen Covey discusses the concept of the "emotional bank account." Like a regular bank account, you make deposits and withdrawals, except instead of money, you use emotions. If you help a friend move furniture, you are making a deposit. If you make time for a conversation with your daughter about something that's important to her, you are making a deposit.

Even with the strongest relationships, you can get your emotional bank account into the red. If you ask a friend for a favor too many times, no matter how good the friendship is, he will eventually begin to feel that you are taking advantage of him. Go to a friend complaining about your life too many times, and he will begin to avoid conversations with you. You are making too many withdrawals from the emotional bank account, and your account is overdrawn.

To strengthen already-strong relationships, focus on making deposits into your emotional bank account. Show kindnesses, both large and small, without being asked. Volunteer to help wherever you can. If the question comes up about why you are being so thoughtful, tell them simply, "I value our relationship, and I want to make sure that you know it."

Of course, this technique is also useful with relationships that may have deteriorated. However, if you start doing favors for someone when your relationship is on rocky ground, they may suspect you of ulterior motives, or of being manipulative. In that case, what you consider deposits, the other person considers withdrawals. Trust must be established before deposits into the emotional bank account can be made.

Finally, look at establishing new relationships. Perhaps there are individuals whom you classify as acquaintances and whom you'd like to know better. (Keep in mind that they likely classify you in the same way, so sudden aggressiveness on your part may surprise them!) But if you already engage them in conversation, ask questions to find out their interests and concerns. Becoming genuinely interested in other people is the key to forming new relationships.

If you are single, and desire a long term relationship, I think it is helpful to describe to yourself the qualities of your perfect mate, and the type of relationship you would like to be in. You are in the driver's seat, and you have the ability to decide for yourself what type of person you will cherish. By having a definite idea of the type of mate you desire, you will automatically attract and notice that type of person.

Always keep in mind the concept of making deposits into the emotional bank account. Deposits only count if they are of value to the other person, and you can only know that if you genuinely care about them.

THE IMPORTANCE OF RELATIONSHIPS

If you view having good relationships as part of your vision, you can see how, despite temporary differences of opinion or viewpoint you might have with someone else, your focus is always on keeping the relationship strong and productive.

What constitutes a "strong and productive" relationship? It's one in which both parties benefit. For example, you would never approach someone to invest in your company if he was not going to earn a profit. You would merely be using that person for selfish personal reasons. However, if you approach a potential partner to offer him a chance to invest, and in return, offer him a solid chance at a good return on his money, both of you benefit from the relationship. It would be productive.

If you approach a new relationship with only your own goals in mind, then it is doomed to fail. A productive relationship requires balance to survive and thrive. Of course you have objectives that you want to accomplish, but they can not be your primary motivation. Benefits to the other person have to be established early on for a relationship to take hold.

In a productive relationship, the interests of both parties are advanced. In the case of the business partner mentioned above, it was his financial wellbeing that was advanced. For others, it may be emotional wellbeing that is improved.

To improve another person's emotional wellbeing, you must be the type of person who fosters positive emotions. The other person, in turn, fosters your emotional wellbeing. In a productive relationship, whether financial or emotional, your interaction is *win-win*. Everyone benefits.

Such relationships are much more fulfilling when you share *core values* with the other person. Basic concepts like honesty, trust, respect, and communication must be important to both of you. When you share values, then you hold similar outlooks on life. The bonds that connect you are strong.

This doesn't mean that you have to agree with every opinion that the other person holds. People of integrity can hold different beliefs on any topic, even such hot-button issues as politics or religion. When you share core values, these differences can be discussed without threatening the relationship. Differences can be acknowledged and respected.

In a fulfilling, productive relationship, the relationship itself takes primary importance. Differences can be discussed without either person feeling diminished or threatened. Of course, this can only happen when each party respects the other. Holding the individual in high regard is a key requirement for a strong relationship. When you have that kind of regard for someone, personal attacks are not even a consideration. The relationship takes priority.

Once you have established boundaries that you both can respect, a relationship of this kind recharges and revitalizes you. When you agree on something, you feel better and both your interests are advanced. When you agreeably disagree, you are presented with a different viewpoint that may open your own mind to new possibilities. You advance because your vision and your options have expanded.

It's a great idea to establish goals around your major relationships, such as family. Family goals might include planning a seaside vacation or saving for a child's education. With your spouse, it might mean planning the number of children you want to have. You can use this technique for any number and levels of activities, from planning to buy a home to setting goals for your personal time together.

THE IMPORTANCE OF TRUST

Strong, productive relationships can only exist if plenty of trust exists between the parties. Each party can depend on the strength, honesty, integrity, and abilities of the other. Think of the people you know. Aren't there some people that you are *positive* that you can count on for certain things? Aren't there others you aren't as sure of? With which people do you have the better relationships?

Whether in business or in your personal life, quality relationships depend on the level of trust that the participants have in each other. The higher the level of trust, the greater the quality of the relationship. Even with acquaintances where interactions are on a more superficial level, even a small level of trust adds to the quality of the relationship.

Deep, rich friendships usually take many years to mature and reach this level. The patterns of trust have been built progressively, each person making small adjustments and compensations for the idiosyncrasies of the other. Lower levels of trust are built upon until the friendship stands firmly entrenched. Time and effort provide strength and depth to a friendship.

How do you go about building trust? By being trustworthy—that is, being *worthy* of trust. You achieve this worthiness by adhering to traditional standards of honor. Be honest, keep your word, and show respect for the other person. These are traits that are under your complete control in a relationship. No one else has control over your honor.

You show the value that you put in a relationship by how well you keep your commitments to the other person. What you place before those commitments tells the other person where they stand with you. For example, let's say that you make a lunch date with a friend. Half an hour before the time to meet them, your boss asks you if you want to have lunch with him. No clients or business are involved, it's just the boss wanting to be sociable.

If you cancel the date with your friend, you are telling him that you have other plans—even ones as commonplace as the situation described—that you place above him. If, on the other hand, you tell your boss that you have a prior commitment, the friend knows that you have placed him above other options.

There is no chart or graph to determine when or under what circumstances you should keep or break a commitment with a friend. Every broken commitment is a withdrawal from the emotional bank account, and too many withdrawals can destroy trust. Honoring commitments both large and small, on the other hand, is a huge deposit in the account, and a relationship will flourish with that kind of investment.

The main thing to remember in any relationship is that trust can not be assumed automatically. It must be earned. The only way to earn trust is to honor the relationship and to follow the fundamental principles of honor and decency.

EFFECTIVE COMMUNICATION IN RELATIONSHIPS

We've all heard about how important "communication" is to us. *Lack of communication is one of the major causes of relationship problems.* Communication is important in the workplace, at home, and in public: there sometimes seems to be more talk about communication than about anything else!

First of all, what's the definition of communication? When we talk to people at work or at home, aren't we "communicating"? Unfortunately, the answer is *probably not*. If you have misunderstandings, misinterpretations, or times when one of you simply doesn't "get" what the other is saying, then you're not really communicating.

Communication is *when the meaning of what you want to convey to another person is completely and accurately transmitted and received*. Although it sounds simple, the definition hides a slew of possible obstacles to communication. Otherwise we would all be master communicators, and there would never be any misunderstandings.

Simply the word "meaning," for example, holds massive amounts of subtext. There are the words you speak (if you're speaking), plus what the words mean to the person with whom you're communicating. Even if you just stop there, you run into problems. A single word can mean different things to different people, based on their experiences, perceptions, and point of view. Ask several people how they define the words "truth" or "good" and you will get an idea of the complexities involved. Multiply your sampling by every word in your vocabulary and you will have an idea of how big a task it is to communicate effectively.

It's clear, then, that communication is more than simply talking and listening. Although effectively using those two skills will improve your communication drastically, they are just a small part of the arsenal you can bring to good communication. Unfortunately, most people have not even mastered these two skills. Because we learn these skills at an early age, we think good speaking and good listening come naturally, when nothing could be further from the truth.

We use communication to transmit ideas. However, even two people who are extremely close, who have a great affinity for one another, can have communication breakdown sometimes, when they simply can't understand one another. The idea—the meaning, the entire package of emotions, images, consequences and causes—simply isn't coming through clearly.

One of the great stories of the Bible is the story of the Tower of Babel. In the world after the flood, everyone spoke one language. The citizens of Babylon began to build a tower so immense it would reach into the heavens. God was displeased with this development, a brazen display of man's hubris, so He confused their languages and scattered them across the earth.

It wasn't a bolt of lightning that destroyed everything, or some other cataclysmic display of power. People simply became unable to understand one another. There are many organizations and companies that suffer from similar situations: an office full of people, yet no one really understands what the others are doing.

One point so far should be obvious: perfect communication is a tough, almost impossible goal. Fortunately, perfection is not necessary in order to make progress and to move forward. All the wonders of modern civilization were accomplished by imperfect human beings, imperfectly communicating. Everything, from the Great Pyramid of Egypt to the Eiffel Tower to micro-circuitry, was created using imperfect communication. Not only has communication helped build civilization, it has made civilization possible.

Communication defines relationships. When a couple is having problems, what's one of the first signs? A breakdown in communication. When someone close to us is unnaturally quiet, we notice and ask them what's wrong. In arguments, you may scream or say things you don't mean—both examples of poor communication.

On the other hand, when your relationship with another person is strong and secure, you can talk about subjects that are sensitive. You can discuss problems quietly and rationally to work together to find an answer. Nuances of meaning and emotion are understood easily because of the bond you share. Simply making eye contact conveys a lot of information.

One of the major goals of good communication is to prevent misunderstandings. We unnecessarily complicate our lives because of garbled messages. Someone close to us may get his or her feelings hurt because of a misunderstanding. Friendships break up because one friend misunderstands something the other has said.

Communicating effectively can prevent or eliminate problems. If we understand one another, and have a clear idea of what someone else is saying, then we react according to the information we are given. If there is poor communication, then we are reacting according to incorrect information—the information we *thought* we received. And because of the poor communication, the original communicator never realizes something is wrong until it's too late.

With this information, then, it becomes apparent that if we communicate effectively, eliminating misunderstandings and eliminating problems, we will work more effectively and efficiently. We can move in a straight line directly from problem to solution. Even better, we can move directly to those activities that provide the best return on invested time and energy: the time and energy that would be wasted with poor communication.

If we recognize that effective communication is the ability *of all parties involved* to convey information clearly and unambiguously, certain points become evident. First of all, listening is as important as speaking, if not more so. As has been pointed out so often, we have two ears and one mouth, and we should use those tools in the same proportion.

We have to pay attention when another person is speaking (or communicating in whatever way), because without our attention, there is a greater chance that miscommunication will occur. While listening attentively won't guarantee that there will be no misunderstanding, it greatly improves the odds of a successful communication between the sender and the receiver.

A great way to ensure effective communication is to check for understanding during a conversation by seeking feedback. During any conversation, there should be a series of clues sent back to the speaker from the listener, indicating that the latter understands. If the speaker feels that there may be a gap in understanding, then he needs to seek feedback to confirm what has been said.

Seeking feedback means *actively* looking for signs that the listener understands. It means being observant and alert for all of the normal signs of comprehension that the other person exhibits. It means looking for the emotional impact that the conversation is having on the other person.

The most difficult conversations that we have, and the ones that are most often mishandled, occur when the subject matter is controversial or critical, and when emotions are high. It is ironic that when the subject matter is most important, our communicating abilities deteriorate. Our feelings take over, and we focus on our own emotional response rather than on communicating.

In the book *Crucial Conversations: Tools for Talking When Stakes are High*, the authors discuss the concept of *safety* in a conversation. They point out that the free flow of ideas and information in a dialogue can only happen when both parties feel safe. The higher the safety level, the greater the flow of ideas. Many times we engage in conversations concerned that we will be attacked or humiliated. We focus so much on our own emotions that we can't concentrate on the communication. The lower the safety level (and the higher the level of fear), the slower the flow of ideas.

The authors recommend that you be aware of the "safety level" in a conversation, and when you sense that the other person is beginning to feel unsafe, based on the feedback that you've looked for, or when you begin to feel unsafe yourself, take a moment to make sure that both of you feel safe before continuing. This can be as simple as reassuring the other person of their value to you.

With that in mind, it's important to prepare the environment for the conversation. If there is a high level of tension in the air, the conversation will be more difficult. The conditions are automatically against effective communication. You can prepare the environment by reassuring the other person beforehand, and approaching the conversation with heightened awareness of the other person's emotional state, as well as your own.

There are obviously many different types of communication. In fact, communication is the one area that has exploded with possibilities over the last decade. The rise of the internet, itself just a more comprehensive form of communication, and of microelectronics, has created a boom in electronic communication.

At its most fundamental level, however, most communication is a face-to-face conversation between two people. In a simple conversation, there are a number of methods of communication being used. First, the words being spoken. Each word has a particular dictionary definition, or *denotation.*

But words also have *connotation,* the second meaning or subtext that accompanies the denotation. The connotation of language refers to the emotional impact that the word causes in the listener. Connotation also refers to experiences with the word that have gone on before. For example, a family might know of a particular food that the children don't like, which, when speaking to one another, becomes a code word for food they don't enjoy.

Along with words, part of a conversation is the voice that each speaker uses. The tone, volume, speed of speech, rate of breathing—all of these are indications that listeners pay attention to in order to determine the speaker's meaning. You need to be aware of your own voice and how it affects other people when you speak. The variety of factors that determine your voice are some of the factors in a conversation that you can control.

Another factor in a conversation is your body language. Entire books have been written on interpreting body language, but most people lack the expertise to be competent in understanding subtle physical cues. Many people use lots of gestures and body movements to convey meaning when they speak—things picked up naturally or culturally—and can throw out false cues to people not adept at reading body language.

With written communication, of course, such factors as body language are not important. The choice of words was once a major part of written communication, but in this era of e-mail, IMs, and text messages, word usage has become secondary to electronic shorthand. Still, when sending a written communication, think of the context in which the receiver will see the message and what the impact of the particular words may be.

Listening effectively is one of the most important aspects of good communication. When you're listening attentively, you indicate that you are receptive, ready to understand what the other person is saying. It shows a preparedness to actually hear his or her point of view. One of the recommended habits in Stephen Covey's book, *The 7 Habits of Highly Effective People,* is: "Seek first to understand, and then to be understood." As you enter into a dialogue with another person, remember the basics—listen for emotion and subtext to what the other person is saying. Listen for *connotation* as well as *denotation.*

When it is your turn to speak, try to augment the effectiveness of your communication by considering the other person's listening style. That means you have to *talk for understanding*. When you talk for understanding, you complement the way the other person listens and processes information. You look for feedback in emotion, as well as in words and meaning.

What happens when you don't talk for understanding? You increase the risk of misunderstanding and incomprehension. You wind up feeling that what you said "went in one ear and out the other." Such a conversation frustrates both you and the person you're speaking to.

When you make the effort to talk for understanding, you show sympathy for the listener, as well as respect. You are giving equality to both sides of the dialogue, ensuring that the matter being discussed is resolved in the most satisfactory manner. When you take into consideration the way the other person processes information, or learns, it shows that you think enough of them and of the situation that you are giving them serious attention.

In today's international business environment, and with international travel becoming more and more commonplace, we have more opportunities than ever before to communicate with people from other cultures. It's important that we consider the differences in cultures when communicating with others in this setting. Misunderstandings can arise when we ignore cultural differences in communication styles. Simple things such as shaking hands or bowing, or even paying someone a compliment on his or her hairstyle, can be misinterpreted.

In relationships, communication means much more than just understanding the other person's words. It means understanding the other person's point of view, and seeing *why* he says or does certain things. It also means helping him understand your point of view, so that he can see the *why* of your own actions. You understand one another's strengths and vulnerabilities.

When we speak of vulnerabilities, we're talking about the soft emotional spots that each of us possesses. In a strong relationship, one partner is understanding and can support the other when their vulnerability shows. For those who have lost their parents, Mothers' Day or Fathers' Day may be upsetting emotionally. The emotions may express themselves as bouts of anger, sadness, withdrawal, or any combination of those or other emotions. Understanding the vulnerability of a person under these or similar circumstances is an indication of a strong relationship.

Emotions often express themselves in indirect ways. Through sincere interest in, and care for, another person, you can learn and forgive these expressions when they happen. An important point I'd like you to remember is that *a relationship is more than a single episode of less-than-perfect behavior.* The best relationships survive these episodes.

Each of us has our own strengths and weaknesses. A strong relationship acknowledges each person's weaknesses and compensates for them. If one of you lacks physical strength, you neither expect nor ask that person to do something that would require him to exhibit great physical strength. You acknowledge that particular weakness, and help him lift weights too heavy for him.

Forgiveness of weaknesses does not mean that you put up with behavior that violates your beliefs or values. If you have a friend who engages in immoral behavior (based on the values that you believe you have in common), the reason for that weakness should be addressed. However, a strong relationship also means that you care enough for the other person that an unusual display of weakness does not threaten the relationship.

When things go wrong, be prepared to forgive and to put mistakes in the past. Rather than dwelling on mistakes and misunderstandings which will put us in a negative frame of mind, have a mindset of finding solutions. This will switch the mood and create a positive to work toward.

Whenever we dwell on negative situations, focusing on the wrong that has been done, we are actually inviting and recognizing other negative occurrences into our lives. Maintaining a positive outlook doesn't mean sticking your head in the sand and not noticing when things are going sideways. It means looking for a solution with a positive frame of mind and believing that there is a solution to be found. By doing this, we can recognize and attract positive ideas and situations.

Likewise, when we have built a high level of trust, human imperfections don't threaten us. After all, life is full of unpredictable moments. A friend or acquaintance may break his word or fail to honor a commitment. With a high level of trust, our reaction is to support the other person, rather than cast blame.

Obviously, strong relationships are of a high quality. They contain a high level of trust, and we protect them whenever we can. It's important to recognize the weaknesses, imperfections and vulnerabilities of the other person, but it's also important to be willing to accept the person's support when you show these same traits. You're human, too, and although it's admirable to aim for perfection, it's not realistic. You will occasionally fall short yourself.

At such times, you need to be able to depend on the other person. I mean this not only in the sense that they are dependable, but that you are honest enough with yourself to accept their help when offered. Pride is one of the worst killers of relationships—*Pride goeth before a fall*—and when someone with whom you have a strong, quality relationship offers you help, you know that it's for the right motives.

PROFESSIONAL RELATIONSHIPS

On the most pragmatic level, customers prefer to do business with people they like. If they derive pleasure from dealing with you, your business is likely to prosper. If likeability were the only criteria, though, service, quality and dependability wouldn't matter. For anyone who has been in business more than ten minutes, that thought sounds ridiculous. It takes much more than surface charm to get and keep a customer's business.

Whatever business you're in, the key to success is selling *yourself.* Your customers absolutely have to believe that you have their interests in mind when you approach them. If you follow the guidelines described earlier and show honesty, integrity, and dependability when dealing with your customers, they will be more receptive to ideas you may present to them.

Because those traits are not so common today, even old fashioned, when you display such virtues you will stand out from most of the people they know. *Quality* is the term that comes to mind, and quality people are always attractive. That is, other people will be attracted to you when you have shown your worth to them.

What this means is that while you always want to put your best foot forward when describing your product or service, you should never misrepresent or lie. Such actions poison a relationship, and when discovered, they destroy trust that can never be fully restored. When you place your customers' concerns at the same level as your own, and commit to a win-win relationship, you set the bar high, and you should strive to always rise to that level.

Relationships are critical to the efficient functioning of a company, whether it is on an assembly line or in a front office. You can create a culture of trust, cooperation, and high standards. Simple plans introduced with genuine care for the people involved work wonders. Clearly communicated goals for individual and team performance can be developed, along with award and recognition programs.

Here are some questions to ask yourself as you consider your relationships:

Do I have fulfilling, supportive relationships in my life?

Am I the kind of friend, lover, parent, coworker, employee or employer that I want to be?

What are the qualities I look for in my various relationships?

What am I prepared to offer in return?

Do I dwell on negative situations for prolonged periods of time? Or do I immediately begin to look for a positive outcome and focus on that?

MY PROMISE

I promise…

- to forgive myself and those around me for mistakes made in the past
- to move forward with a spirit of understanding and cooperation
- to bring the best that is in me to all of my relationships
- to honour my own needs as well as those of others in my relationships, and
- to listen to others effectively.

CHAPTER SEVEN
—Your Body, Your Temple—

CHAPTER SEVEN
—*Your Body, Your Temple*—

Whenever someone writes a book like this one, the reader often focuses on mental exercises, introspection, and using his or her brain in the best way possible. This is all as it should be, because all creation begins in the mind first. However, if we focus on the mental aspects of self improvement *exclusively*, we neglect one important tool: our bodies.

Although every improvement in your life begins with an idea, the actual execution of that idea depends on your actions. The effectiveness of those actions, and the efficiency with which you execute them, depends on your body. The more efficiently your body works, the more efficiently you can do the things you need and want to do.

The importance of physical health and wellbeing stems from the interrelation of the different aspects of your life. The mind-body connection has been well-documented. A healthy body helps produce a healthy mind, which in turn benefits physical health. (Or is it the other way around?) This is like the question of which came first, the chicken or the egg. The two are so interrelated that the cycle has no beginning and no end. It's a cycle that it benefits you to pay attention to.

This chapter discusses physical health, and different things you can do to improve your health. However, I am not a physician. Everything I mention in this chapter is a general guide only. If you have any special health concerns, take those into consideration before implementing any of the tips in this chapter. **Consult a medical professional before beginning any new diet or exercise regimen.**

As I mentioned earlier, your body is a tool with which you express the ideas your mind creates. Picasso had to physically hold a paintbrush to paint his masterpieces. The greatest physical specimens of the human race have always had to decide what they wanted to do first, and then use their bodies to accomplish their goals.

It is absolutely vital that, at the very least, you set some sort of optimal or ideal health goal. Decide the specifics yourself, based on your existing health, situation, and resources. Having a clear mental picture of what your ideal health would be like makes it more likely that you will progress toward that ideal.

Remember: when our physical health suffers, everything else in our lives can suffer. Our relationships, our finances, our employment, and our spiritual and religious beliefs can be questioned. Our own self-awareness can be challenged.

What are the various factors affecting your physical health? **There are several things to keep in mind:**

- Emotions
- Rest
- Diet
- Exercise
- Environment
- Awareness

Emotions. The mind-body connection that I spoke of earlier is one that often catches people by surprise. With the increasingly high level of stress and anxiety in today's world, we are also seeing a rise in stress-related illnesses. Stomach and digestive problems, hypertension (high blood pressure), and stress-related headaches are just a few of the maladies that are related to emotional turmoil.

On the other hand, positive emotions can contribute to your wellness. One of the most famous documented cases was related by writer Norman Cousins in his book, *Anatomy of an Illness (as Perceived by the Patient.)* Cousins was an editor for the New York Evening Post and the Saturday Review. At one point, he was diagnosed with a debilitating form of arthritis which left him bedridden and in constant pain. Doctors were forced to give him large doses of painkillers to help relieve his suffering. As his condition worsened, he was told that he had little chance of surviving. Cousins decided to take his treatment into his own hands.

Cousins checked out of the hospital and into a hotel. He had read about the benefits of Vitamin C, so he started taking large doses intravenously. Additionally, he began to read positive literature, filling his mind with messages of hope, faith and love. He added laughter to his treatment by watching old Marx Brothers movies. Cousins recounted his experience: "I made the joyous discovery that ten minutes of genuine belly laughter had an anesthetic effect, and would give me at least two hours of pain-free sleep. When the pain-killing effect of the laughter wore off, we would switch on the motion picture projector again." Norman Cousins went on to live several years longer than his doctors had predicted.

Admittedly, Cousins was in an abnormal situation, facing life or death in the hospital. However, while his condition was acute, many people enduring stress on a daily basis are also suffering the ill effects of negative emotions. Controlling your emotional state—in other words, accentuating the positive and eliminating the negative, as the old song goes—can provide you with relief from many illnesses and simply feeling bad all the time.

Rest. Rest, in the form of deep, replenishing sleep, is one of the most neglected aspects of physical health. These days we seem to want to cram as much activity as possible into our days, trimming the time we sleep shorter and shorter. According to the National Sleep Foundation, the average adult needs about eight hours of sleep a night (although individual sleep needs may vary.) Because of our lifestyles, many people regularly get as little as five or six hours.

Although a short-term episode of insomnia is generally nothing to worry about, long-term sleep deprivation can cause severe problems. The Harvard Medical School identified several different areas in which a lack of restful sleep can cause severe problems.

Learning and memory. According to research, restful sleep can help you learn and retain information better. In studies, subjects who slept after learning a task retained the skills better.

Metabolism and weight. Lack of sleep can disturb the levels of the body's hormones, affecting both appetite and the way the body processes and stores carbohydrates.

Safety. Sleepiness can cause someone to take "mini-naps" lasting five or ten seconds. During this time, the person is completely asleep, but doesn't know it. Imagine if this were to happen while you were driving or performing some other dangerous activity. Many traffic accidents happen for this very reason.

Mood. Besides leaving you too exhausted to do the activities you enjoy doing, lack of sleep can result in irritability, impatience, moodiness, and interfere with your ability to concentrate.

Cardiovascular health. Sleep loss has been linked to hypertension, irregular heartbeat, and increases in the body's stress hormones.

Disease. Sleep deprivation affects the body's immune system. The body's process for producing disease-fighting cells may be altered.

On the other hand, haven't you woken up after a good night's sleep feeling rested and energetic, ready to take on the world? The restorative magic of sleep is simple, proven, and easily available to anyone who chooses to pursue it. By avoiding the lure of squeezing out leisure or work time from sleep time, you can actually improve the quality of your day and the quality of your work.

Here are a few tips that can help you get a better night's sleep:

- Set a definite bed time and time to wake up.
- Avoid alcohol, caffeine or heavy meals for several hours before bed time.
- Make your bedroom a relaxing place. Try for a dark, comfortable environment.
- Avoid taking your worries to bed. Keep a notepad by your bedside to write out any thoughts, ideas, and errands for the next day.
- Develop a pre-sleep routine. A warm bath or a few minutes of reading helps you make the transition from "awake time" to "sleep time."

Diet. It's amazing in our society that so much conflicting information can exist about what we eat. The bookstore shelves sag under the weight of all the diet books promising to help us lose weight, control disease, or otherwise make us healthier and happier. Additionally, a plethora of cookbooks exist for those of us wishing to prepare meals in any number of styles.

It's clear that a lot is going on when it comes to what we eat. If you're feeling confused about your diet, it can help if you cut through all the clutter and get a grasp of the situation. First of all, let's define what is meant by the word "diet." Rather than being a special regimen of particular foods you eat or don't eat for a short time to accomplish a particular purpose, your diet is simply *the food that you usually eat.*

At its most basic level, food is fuel for your body. Just as an automobile needs fuel to operate, so does your body. The food you eat is converted to energy that powers you through the day. That energy conversion is where the word *calorie* comes in. Everything you eat is measured in calories, or amount of energy it provides.

At the same time, your body's energy expenditures— everything from breathing and keeping your heart beating to walking up stairs or running a marathon—are also measured in calories. If you take in more fuel than you burn, your body stores that excess fuel as fat tissue.

Some foods we eat help our body function better than other foods do. Our bodies are much more complex than an automobile. Our brains, muscles, bones and other tissue require different nutrients to help us function. If our diet is deficient in any of the required nutrients, the body functions less efficiently. If the deficiency becomes too severe, the body may even break down.

What we look for in a diet is one that provides the energy we need, and also helps our bodies function at the highest level. The good news is, as complicated as that may sound, it's simple to accomplish. (Note: Health conditions such as diabetes or food-specific allergies place special dietary restrictions on some people. The following information is of a general nature and not intended for those with such conditions.)

When it comes to providing nutrition, most experts agree that we need to eat a lot of fresh fruits and vegetables. As a group, they provide many of the nutrients we need for our bodies to function at the highest level. (Vegetarians might argue that they provide *all* the nutrients we need.)

Some people feel that organic fruits and vegetables, grown under special conditions, usually without the use of any chemicals, provide the best nutrition. If you feel that way, please, indulge yourself. For other people, the higher cost of organic foods is prohibitive. Whether you decide to go organic or not, adding more fresh fruit and vegetables to your diet can only help.

What about meat? In general, experts agree that eating lean cuts of meat in moderate amounts provides nutrients such as protein and iron. Sticking with lean meat also avoids some of the fears of higher cholesterol or excess calories. Adding regular servings of fish to your diet also adds other nutrients such as omega-3 fatty acids.

Add grains and cereals to your diet (most experts recommend whole grains), and you have the fundamentals of an eating program that will help you function most effectively. Keep an eye on your servings so that you don't take in more calories than you need, and you will find yourself with added energy and improved health.

Exercise. Did you notice how I sneakily slipped in the phrase "don't take in more calories than you need" just now? I didn't do it to stump you (*how in the world are you supposed to know how many calories you need?*), but because of the relationship between diet and exercise.

As I mentioned earlier, food provides energy, measured in calories. All of our body's activities burn energy, and that process is also measured in calories. If we take in more calories than we expend, the body stores them. If we take in fewer calories than we expend, the body uses existing tissue as fuel, and we lose weight.

Generally, in our culture, we don't suffer from not getting enough calories. In fact, we consume many more calories than we need. Obesity has become a health issue of such proportions that the medical community has begun addressing it. Children have become more obese, with the accompanying ailments.

To live a healthier, more satisfying life, a balance of diet and exercise provides the best answer. A good diet such as the one mentioned above provides the fuel and nutrients. What, then, constitutes good exercise?

First of all, exercise is not necessarily running or lifting weights, although both of those activities can be very beneficial. Exercise is any activity that requires you to exert your body in some way. Gardening, doing housework or playing with your children can be exercise. They burn calories and involve bodily movement.

Many people, however, don't get enough exercise. We live sedentary lifestyles, sitting most of the day in an office, then collapsing onto the couch in front of the television when we get home. Add in the extra calories that we're eating, and you see the recipe for an obesity epidemic.

If you decide that you want to add exercise to your life, focus on three areas: cardiovascular exercise, strength training, and flexibility.

Cardiovascular exercise is any activity that makes your heart beat fast for extended periods of time. Regular cardiovascular exercise strengthens the heart and helps keep your blood vessels healthy. Walking, running, cycling, or swimming are great ways to get your heart pumping. You can also try dancing, boxing, aerobics classes, or jumping rope. Any activity lasting at least twenty minutes that makes your heart pump and makes you sweat is great.

If you are out of shape, then walking across the room may make your heart beat hard. If that's the case, then walking across the room can be considered cardiovascular exercise for you. The key to a good cardio exercise is to find one you enjoy and that you can continue to do for long periods of time. One of the best forms of exercise is walking.

Enjoyment may be the most important word in the exercise world. Walking as an exercise doesn't mean finding a track and walking in circles for an hour, though it can if that's what you enjoy. Instead, it may mean holding hands with a loved one and taking a stroll through a park. It may mean walking on the beach with your children looking for shells. It may mean strapping on a backpack and walking through the forest at a national park. Find something that you enjoy and do it.

Right off the bat, you may be surprised that you can enjoy exercise. Or, more accurately, exercise while you do something you enjoy. Walking is a great tool for starting out because you can do it at your own pace. The main thing is that you start moving your body through space, use your muscles, especially the large muscles of the lower body, and get blood pumping through your system again.

You likely will soon find that casually strolling no longer makes your heart beat faster or makes you breathe hard. Your body will have adapted to the level of activity that you have asked it to do. At this point, to achieve maximum benefit from cardio exercise, you need to add more intensity to your workout. (Yes, what you've been doing is considered a workout, even though you've been engaging in activities you enjoy. See how easy this can be?) You can start moving faster, start carrying light weights—hand weights or a backpack full of books will do—or find hilly terrain to walk up.

Walking is an activity that almost anyone can do, but clearly there are many other exercises that can be called cardio. Running is good exercise, but can be hard on your joints. Swimming is another excellent cardio exercise that can get your heart rate up without any strain on your joints. However, swimming requires a place to swim and some preparation. If you have access to a body of water or a swimming pool, you're in luck.

Almost anything can be cardio, if you engage in it vigorously enough. Riding a bike, jumping a rope, calisthenics—find something you enjoy and do it. Keep in mind your level of exertion and your level of pleasure while engaged in an activity, and you will soon find that cardio is not as intimidating as you thought.

If you decide that you really want to up the intensity level, consider joining an aerobics class. You're no longer limited to the calisthenics and moves you learned in gym class; you can now try aerobic martial arts, boxing, or other interesting activities. A good instructor will work with you to get the most out of each workout, and you'll have the camaraderie of exercising among others who have the same goals.

Cardiovascular exercises are also called *aerobic exercises.* "Aerobic" means the activity requires air, so your breathing is very important during aerobic exercise. The heart and the lungs work together in a wonderful way. The lungs bring air, or more importantly, oxygen, into the body when you breathe in. Blood vessels surround the lungs, and the moving blood cells capture the oxygen from the air in the lungs and transport it to the rest of the body. The blood carries waste products such as carbon dioxide back to the lungs, where it is exhaled.

Exercises that make your lungs and heart work together in this miraculous process will benefit both your lungs and your heart. For this reason, cardio exercise is considered *maintenance exercise*: it helps you maintain a healthy heart and lungs. Cardio in fact helps the entire circulatory system do its job better.

Cardio is considered one of the three main components of exercise. The other two, strength and flexibility, can be called *performance exercises* because although they help overall health in a variety of ways, their primary benefit is in helping you do the things you want to do physically on a daily basis.

Strength training doesn't necessarily mean working to become the next Arnold Schwarzenegger. What you're looking for is not big muscles, but having enough strength to function in your daily life. You might need to lift your grandchildren, open a jar, or move boxes. Instead of becoming a bodybuilder, your goal could be to maintain functional strength.

Strength (or power) training helps you move the things you want to move. For some people, what they want to move most is their own body. Think about the young mother who has to pick up her thirty pound toddler dozens of times a day, or who has to carry groceries in from the car to the house. Although she may not consider herself a powerful person, she is using the strength in her muscles to perform her daily tasks.

If we let our bodies become so weak that we can no longer pick up our children or carry in sacks of groceries, we can't enjoy life to the fullest. When you can't do your normal work, it makes it more difficult to do the physical things you enjoy, like playing basketball with friends or walking in the park with a loved one.

To increase your strength, you'll have to exert your muscles. In this case, however, you won't be moving your body through space, you'll be using your muscles to move other things. More importantly, you won't be working on your breathing (although proper breathing technique is always important). To increase your strength, you have to engage your muscles in *resistance training*.

Resistance training is best described as pushing something that feels as though it's pushing back, or resisting. Most people think of lifting weights when they think of resistance training, and weightlifting is a great way to increase your strength. Lifting weights doesn't mean you have to lift so much weight that the bar bends, like you see on television. A few hand weights and light dumbbells may be just what you need.

If you decide to lift weights, you have many options. You can join a gym that has a variety of different weights and machines. This option gives you the maximum number of options for pursuing resistance training. You'll see small weights that can be held in your hand: dumbbells. You'll see heavier weights that attach to a bar that requires both hands to hold: barbells.

You may also see machines that have different kinds of weights. Check with the trainer at your gym to find out how to use all these machines. Many of them isolate particular muscles for you to exercise, while others work multiple groups of muscles at a time. Be careful and observe all safety rules and guidelines when using weight machines. Although they are designed to provide maximum security, any time you're dealing with heavy weights and metal there is potential for getting hurt.

Some people, especially women, worry about getting big muscles from lifting weights. They see bodybuilders in the movies and on television, and don't want to look like that. The good news is, you won't. Bodybuilders work for years to make their muscles that large, with specialized exercises, diets, supplements, and training.

What you will find, though, is that with time and proper workouts, your muscles will become more compact and firm. And, of course, you'll become stronger. So, you ask, what's the deal with the big muscles? How do you get those? There's a saying in the weightlifting world: "Lift big, get big." In other words, you have to lift heavy weights to get big muscles.

A word of explanation is in order. You can lift weights, and work your muscles with weights, in two different ways. You can either lift light weights multiple times, or lift heavy weights a few times. Both of these options accomplish the goal of working the muscles to exhaustion.

Using light weights has many benefits. First of all, you are less likely to injure yourself by using light weights. Doing more repetitions will lead to greater strength and firmer muscles. You will receive all the benefits of weightlifting, except one: big muscles.

When you lift heavy weights, you are actually rupturing muscle fibers. These fibers repair themselves and become stronger and bigger. Many chemicals and hormones in the body, mainly testosterone, affect the rate of growth and increased strength. Muscles will become sore from the ruptured fibers, and it's during this sore period after the weightlifting session that muscles repair themselves and grow. A rest period of at least 48 hours is necessary for the muscle to heal properly. That's why weightlifters who lift this way only work a muscle group two or three times a week.

Weightlifting is not the only form of resistance training you can do. Many people do resistance training with their own body weight. If you've ever done a chin-up or a push-up, you've done resistance training the old fashioned way. The clear advantage of body weight training is that you don't need any special equipment.

Another resistance exercise that doesn't require equipment is isometric training. Isometrics don't involve movement; you are simply "straining" a muscle against something that doesn't move. For example, if you press your palms together as hard as you can, you are exerting your muscles, although nothing moves. You might press down against a table, or push against a door frame (as long as you're not moving your body away.)

A resistance exercise that requires only a simple piece of equipment involves rubber bands or tubes. These are specialized bands or tubes that you loop around one part of your body while pulling with another part. Portable, flexible, and handy, these tools are often used by travelers in their hotel rooms when other exercise options are not available.

Another place to do resistance exercise is in the water. Have you ever noticed how hard it is to move when you're body is under water? That's because of the resistance the water offers against your body. Many exercise centers offer water exercise classes as a way to incorporate resistance training.

Water exercises, bands, and isometrics are all good methods of resistance training for senior citizens or those with physical limitations. They offer the benefits of muscle training without the jarring impact that lifting weights may have.

Flexibility is the ability to move your body with a great range of motion. Sometimes, either because of age or lifestyle, we become stiff and unable to move as efficiently as we'd like. That stiffness limits how much we can do, both at work and in our leisure time. If you've ever sat out a game with your children or grandchildren because you're too stiff, you know how important flexibility can be.

Several different activities can help you increase your flexibility. Simply stretching can provide you with an increase range of motion. There are many activities designed to focus on improving your flexibility. Chief among these is yoga.

When most of think of yoga, we think of practitioners bending themselves into pretzels. Although some yoga practitioners do have extraordinary flexibility, you don't have to achieve that same level to benefit from yoga. Technically, *yoga* refers to a series of exercises, physical and mental, invented in India. These exercises were to prepare the body and mind spiritually to be ready to accept enlightenment.

The sort of yoga that we normally associate with the word is *hatha yoga*. Although you may discover you want to pursue yoga more deeply, the main reason we use it at first is to increase flexibility. Yoga is a series of small, subtle movements done with full concentration. In yoga classes, a calm, relaxed state of mind is encouraged, and often, soft music is played.

If you choose to attend a yoga class, find a class for beginners and try to visit the class first to see how the instructor works. A good instructor will be calm, encouraging, and helpful. You will likely see students at all different levels, and most of them are there for the same reason you are.

A benefit you will likely see after doing yoga for a while is a more relaxed frame of mind. Take the opportunity in your classes to leave the outside world behind and focus entirely on your movement and breathing. Although all forms of exercise have multiple benefits, yoga offers a calming influence that can help you.

Other activities that you might engage in to help with your flexibility are dance classes, or even martial arts. Both of these offer you the opportunity to stretch before, during and after class, and you'll soon find that your flexibility increases simply by stretching on a regular basis.

Some nutritional supplements can help flexibility, but the best thing you can do is to add movement to your life. Using your body in a variety of ways will increase your range of motion and coordination, and help you maintain smoothness of movement. Have you ever noticed how dancers move? Or how athletes walk? Their muscles, bones and joints move together in a way that is impossible for people who are out of shape and don't use their bodies.

Regardless of what type of activities you do for exercise, it's important that you do *something*. Choose activities that are fun and give you time to spend with family or friends. Play active games. Whatever you choose to do will help.

Environment. You can spend all the time and effort you want on diet and exercise, but if you are in a toxic environment, you may still suffer physically. Depending on your location and your lifestyle, you may have physical maladies and limitations that restrict how effectively your body does what you want it to do.

While diet and exercise are essentially internal functions, your environment is any of the external factors that contribute to the state of your health. If you live in a large city, air pollution may be an issue. If you live in an old building, hazardous materials such as asbestos can affect your health. Be aware of these factors as much as possible, and take appropriate measures to protect yourself.

One of the biggest environmental issues is cigarette smoking. It's not a moral judgment to recognize that smoking is bad for your health. The message has been out for nearly fifty years that smoking can make you sick or even cause death. If you want to operate at your most effective level, don't smoke.

What if you work or live around smokers? Treat secondhand smoke just as you would any other form of pollution. Take whatever measures you can to protect yourself. If you can talk the smoker into not smoking around you, do it. If you can convince him or her to quit permanently, even better.

Awareness. The most important thing you can do to maintain your best physical health is to be aware. Pay attention to your body and to the world around you. Part of that awareness means visiting your doctor regularly for checkups. You may be perfectly fine physically, and the physician will confirm that. If something is wrong, you can detect it early and get appropriate treatment.

Use your awareness to detect changes in how you feel, and see if you are getting the proper amount of rest and exercise. Determine if you have let your diet get out of whack. Think about how you have felt emotionally, and if that may be affecting you negatively.

Many health organizations, conscious of the importance of awareness and prevention, will proclaim a particular disease, syndrome, or condition as the focus of a particular month, week, or day. For example, the month of January is celebrated as, variously, Cervical Health Awareness Month, National Birth Defects Prevention Month, National Glaucoma Awareness Month, National Radon Action Month, Thyroid Awareness Month, and National Folic Acid Awareness Month!

While these proclamations and campaigns may seem incredibly, even comically, specific, they help make people aware of the particular subject, and provide materials to help people learn about the subject. Much of this material is not easily available otherwise. What's more, many of the people involved in these campaigns are experts in that specific field of knowledge. They are a tremendous resource for information.

Remember that your body is the tool with which you accomplish all the wonderful things you have in your mind. Treat it well, and your body—the only one you will ever have—will carry your dreams as far as you care to go.

Some questions to ask yourself when considering your physical health:

- Do I treat my body with respect, get plenty of rest, exercise, and good nutrition?
- Is there a hobby or pastime that I have wanted to start, but have been procrastinating on?
- Do I allow daily stresses to affect my health?
- Can I adjust my schedule so that I have time for meditation and relaxation on a regular basis?
- What is my body telling me right now?

MY PROMISE

I promise…

- to care for my health and wellbeing daily, knowing that a healthy body is a reflection of a healthy mind, and the vessel and conduit for all the good works I intend on performing; and
- to treat myself to regular exercise, restful sleep, and good nutrition.

CHAPTER EIGHT
—The Wealth Mindset—

CHAPTER EIGHT

—*The Wealth Mindset*—

A fact of life in modern western culture is that we need money. Money is used for a variety of different functions, from purchasing the necessities of life to keeping score on how well we're doing at work. Money can provide us with prestige and status, and can make it possible for us to help other people.

All of these functions are based on *assumptions* about money, not on money itself. Money provides us with purchasing power when we buy groceries at the supermarket. Whether you pay with cash, cheque, or credit card, the store assumes that it will be able to deposit that purchasing power into the bank and use it for its own purposes.

If you earn more than your peers at work, you assume that you are doing a better job (in some fashion or another). When you do a good job, you hope for a raise in pay. If you take that raise and purchase a fancy car, you show your status to the world. If you take the raise and donate more to a charity, you help other people.

The idea of money can get complicated if you let it. Worry about money is one of the most common sources of stress and anxiety today. Fortunately, if you have the right mindset about money, and follow some basic principles and strategies, money can provide for you and your family as well as help others.

THE WEALTH MINDSET

Ask most people today what their first thought is about money and they'll likely respond "There's not enough of it!" Regardless of how much money they have or don't have, the vast majority of people today wish they had more money. It's a common problem that our lifestyles often seem to bubble up and strain our income. There never seems to be "enough."

Unfortunately, for some people this leads to jealousy of others who have more money. Somehow the idea becomes implanted that if *that* person has more, it takes away from *me*. The thought that there is some kind of competition for all the money means that there will be losers and winners, and the winners win at the expense of the losers.

This emotional response ignores the fact that *wealth is not a zero-sum game*. If I read in the newspaper that a professional athlete has been awarded a multi-million dollar contract, does it take money from my pocket? Of course not. I still retain the ability to go out and earn as much money as I can. As long as I provide value to the world, my earning power has not been diminished one iota by someone else's increased earning power.

The universe is abundant with resources and treasure. Another person's fortune, whether good or bad, does not diminish what is available to us. My opportunities and ability to reach my share of the treasure in the universe remain open to me. This is the essence of the *wealth mindset.*

There are two types of payment we receive: psychic income and financial income. Psychic income is hard to measure. It is that wonderful feeling of bliss we experience when we know we have made a contribution to another person, or done the best job we could, or done the right thing.

Financial income, of course, is the monetary compensation you receive. The Law of Compensation is reflected in our financial income. The demand for what you do, your ability to do it, and the difficulty in replacing you, affect the amount of income you will generate.

DISEMPOWERING BELIEFS ABOUT MONEY

Because money is such an emotional subject, we can cripple our ability to earn and keep wealth when we have negative beliefs about it. These beliefs may be summed up by such sayings as, "Money is the root of all evil." These axioms are repeated so often that we don't even think to question them. Let's take a look at some disempowering beliefs about money and wealth.

"Money is the root of all evil." This quote is from the Bible, and thus carries extra weight with many people. The first order of business is to get it right: the actual quote is, "The *love* of money is the root of all evil." (Some say that it can be translated from the original Greek even more accurately as, "The love of money is a root of all sorts of evil.")

Clearly, those with a disproportionate desire for money, placing it above people and relationships, may have a problem. Such a desire can drive an unbalanced individual to commit evil acts. It's probably safe to say, however, that if their problem wasn't money, it would be something else.

"Only bad people are rich." There are bad rich people, and there are good rich people. There are also bad poor people and good poor people. People are people, regardless of the size of their bank accounts. A very large number of wealthy people donate millions of dollars to various charities and organizations that help others. It's probably a safe bet that these people would find some way to help others even if they didn't have that wealth.

According to the book, *The Millionaire Next Door*, most wealthy individuals are those who have worked hard for years, lived within their means, spent less than they earned, and invested their earnings where they would grow. These traits and characteristics don't necessarily make them good people, but would you say that they indicate that they are *bad* people?

"Hoarding money is selfish." As described above, there are some people with wealth who are selfish. There are also many who are incredibly generous. They give large amounts to help others. This is the polar opposite of what is implied with the word "hoarding." If anything, these people have embraced the opportunity to share their wealth with others.

Even for those who choose not to give money away to others, that choice does not make them "selfish." These people have chosen to provide for themselves and their families. Being self-sufficient, they are no burden to anyone else. In most cases, these people pay higher amounts of taxes than those with less wealth. Is it selfish of them to stand on their own two feet and contribute to the general welfare by paying more in taxes?

Here are some other common phrases we hear about money. Think about the times you may have heard them, and if the implication was positive or negative.

- Do you think we are made of money?
- Money doesn't grow on trees.
- Money isn't everything.
- Money can't buy happiness.
- Money will change you.

In all of these cases, the belief that you are somehow doing something "wrong" by wanting to earn more money can paralyze you. Having a focused drive to be good at something for which others will pay you is to be admired. The main thing is to keep your values and priorities in order.

MONEY IS A TOOL

Money is used for many things, as I described at the beginning of the chapter. What money most effectively *is*, though, is a tool. It's something to be used to accomplish other goals. For example, as I mentioned above, it can be used to help others.

One of the most powerful uses of money, of course, is to increase one's assets. When you buy something that increases in value, you purchase an *asset*. You might invest in a business or purchase a stock. You could buy a collectible such as a piece of art that increases in value. When you increase your assets (without a corresponding increase in your debt) you increase your wealth.

Often, people forget that they themselves can be assets. If you invest in going to college, your college degree (according to a 2004 study done by the U.S. Census Bureau) can help you earn nearly twice as much annually as someone who stopped with a high school diploma. Any time you invest in yourself, you are using money as a tool.

On a more mundane level, if you have money on hand, you can take advantage of bargains. Buying items in larger quantities, for example, will let you buy them at a lower per-unit cost. The challenge is that you have to have enough money on hand to purchase the larger quantity. Those who have money on hand and who consistently take advantage of bargains pay less for many items than those who don't save. Money is the tool which allows them to live the same level of lifestyle at a lower cost.

WHAT IS WEALTH?

In the course of all this talk about money and using it as a tool, there is always the danger of getting caught up in the trivial and losing sight of what wealth actually *is*. Of course, it can be defined as the accumulation of assets, but that's sort of dry. Wealth actually means much more than that.

Wealth is *freedom*. If you ever are asked, "How much money is enough?" a great answer would be: *When you don't have to consider your finances as you make most of your daily decisions.* You have the freedom to make decisions based on their own merits.

Some decisions require considering finances, of course: major purchases, investments, etc. If you need to purchase a necessity, though, your first thought should not be, "Can I afford this?" That thought impoverishes you. Your goal should be to achieve enough wealth so that your decision-making process includes considering all the pertinent factors, and *only* those factors.

INCOME VERSUS WEALTH

Most people, as a matter of course, equate "income," the amount of money someone earns, with "wealth." This seemingly logical comparison would work fine if we were able to keep all the money we earn, but as we all know too well, that's simply not the case. Taxes of various amounts are taken from our pay, and then we have our expenses. Rent or mortgage, food, clothing, utilities, loans for cars and vacations, credit cards—these all take a chunk out of our income.

If we define wealth as freedom—the ability to make choices without regards to finances—those chunks taken out of our income make a huge difference. It's not how much you *earn* that matters, it's how much you are able to *keep* that determines how free you are. If you earn a hundred thousand dollars a year, and spend a hundred thousand a year, how much freedom do you truly have?

What I'm talking about here is *balance* and *control*. You're life is out of balance if you find yourself a slave to your lifestyle. If you are forced to neglect your family or other relationships, if you break commitments, if you are forced to drop other obligations, all because you constantly work to earn the money to support your lifestyle, you might think about bringing some balance back into your life.

Think about the things you do with your money. Do you have an emergency fund of some sort, perhaps enough to sustain you in case of a financial disaster? Do you have the right kinds of insurance, in proper amounts? On the other hand, do you spend a large amount of your income on consumables—services, food, or other items that only satisfy your appetite for a short while?

An idea I have is a family version of the macroeconomic theory of "guns and butter." (The original version deals with national defense and production of goods—look it up if you're interested.) My basic premise is this: we spend our money on things that either rise in value (*appreciate*, what I call "guns") or fall in value (depreciate, called "butter.")

Wealthy people, who have a larger net worth, or assets minus debt, spend a large part of their income on appreciable assets (guns) —owning their own business, real estate, and interest-bearing or dividend-earning financial accounts, for example. These types of items increase one's net worth.

People with high-consumption lifestyles spend a large portion of their income on depreciating assets—butter—such as the latest electronic gadgets, recreational equipment and activities and home furnishings.

Consider two families with the same annual income: say, $100,000. Family A lives in a nice home in a nice neighborhood. They take great vacations (paid for with loans or credit cards), drive a brand new car each year (financed, of course), and have a house full of the latest electronic gadgets. At the end of the year, they have all that "stuff," but are buried in debt and anxiety over how they are going to pay for it all.

Family B has savings accounts and other income-earning financial accounts, and owns a small rental property. They live comfortably, but fairly frugally compared to Family A. They don't take extravagant vacations, and they live in a modest home. Although they have exactly the same income, Family B ends the year with an increased net worth: they are wealthier. What debt they have doesn't control them. They have found balance, and with it, freedom.

Control is what it takes to resist the appetite to spend, and to make financial decisions based on your most important values and priorities. We all enjoy having nice things, and I'm not saying that buying them is necessarily a bad thing. It's when we want them so badly that it warps our judgment that we have let the appetite control us. At such times we lack balance.

It helps to establish systems that help you control impulse spending. Some families have a philosophy that any expenditure over a certain amount, say $100, requires a family conversation. Some people put themselves on a weekly allowance that they receive in cash. If they have an impulse to buy something, they do it with that cash; when they're out of cash, they quit spending.

Only you know your own circumstances, and the types of financial decisions that you need to make. Use your imagination to set up controls that work for you. Keep in mind your priorities and values, and mold your decisions to align with them. Not only will you increase your wealth, you'll also find that your stress level will lessen. That's a benefit of establishing balance.

THE ROLE OF DEBT

In light of the current turmoil in the global economy, *debt* has become a dirty word to many people. Debt, in and of itself, is not necessarily a bad thing. It's a tool that can be used to buy a house or a business, or accomplish many other financial goals. Debt simply means borrowing money that you have to pay back. Like any tool, however, it can be misused (as we read in the headlines almost daily.)

Debt can cripple you when it restricts your choices in life. Remember, "wealth" is having freedom, or more choices. When you worry constantly about your debt, wondering if (or even *when*) the bottom will fall out, it's hard to consider yourself wealthy. Digging a hole so deep that you can't see your way out of it not only can lead to bankruptcy, it can also lead to stress, anxiety, and sometimes, health problems and broken relationships.

On the other hand, the wise use of debt is a way to use other people's money (OPM) as leverage to improve your life. For example, very few people buy their first home by paying cash. They get a mortgage from a mortgage lender and make payments. Since your home is usually one of the largest appreciable assets that you can own, prudent borrowing is a smart financial decision. Your home (usually) increases in value, and as you make payments you increase your equity— the amount of money you would put in your pocket if you sold your home and paid off the mortgage. It's a wise use of debt to increase your wealth.

Any time you make a thoughtful, prudent decision to borrow money that you can use to increase your net worth, while staying true to your values, the tool of debt works for you. Do your research, consult experts, realistically consider your financial situation—in other words, think things through—and debt will be helpful to you, rather than a destructive force.

MONEY STRATEGIES

Over the years, those who study finance—both personal and for business—have discovered some strategies that have proven themselves effective time and time again. These strategies are what wealthy people do. As with most things, if you do the same things that successful people do, you increase your chances of being successful yourself.

The following are a few basic strategies. The list is not comprehensive, but if you do these things you will be well on your way to succeeding financially.

Pay yourself first. This strategy is pretty simple, but not always easy to do. This is a BIG issue of control. Before you do anything else with your money, take a portion of it and sock it away in a savings or retirement account. Then, with what's left, pay your bills and make purchases.

This concept is the exact opposite of what most people do. Most people pay their bills before they pay themselves, and they discover that when it comes time to provide for savings—surprise!—there's no money left. They have to pay their bills, they say, and the next month the same thing happens. At the end of the year, they haven't saved anything, and it all seems inevitable.

When you pay yourself first, suddenly you discover that you have to scramble to pay your bills. Guess what? That's a sign that you have too much debt. It's important to establish your priorities and execute them first. *Saving* is a priority; without it you never get off the debt merry-go-round.

Here's a savings program in a nutshell: s*ave 10 to 15% of your gross pay, and live off the rest.* If you do nothing other than follow that one sentence, you will be well ahead of most other people when it comes to saving. Of course, there are ways to maximize the results you get from saving. For example, where should you put the 15% of your pay?

Savings accounts are what most people think of, and they certainly beat nothing, or keeping the cash under your mattress. However, banks pay very little interest on savings accounts, often less than one percent. It's far better to do some research and see if you can find an account that pays more. Banks, credit unions, and other financial institutions offer high-interest accounts. Check around and see if such an account is available to you. Keep an eye out for hidden charges and fees, minimum balance requirements, and other costs associated with a high interest account.

Other places to earn a return on your money are the stock market, bonds, or investment properties. Whatever method you decide to follow, do your research first. The main thing is to establish some sort of savings plan right away.

Ignoring your savings ensures that you focus instead on your debt. Instead of wealth building, you suffer the anxiety caused by constantly worrying about money. When you do think about the future, it's with a sense of despair. Without savings, any small emergency suddenly becomes a crisis.

Live on what you make. This strategy calls for aligning your lifestyle with the amount of income you earn. Before you borrow money, calculate the payments and make sure that you are able to pay back the money without undue strain on your finances.

With persuasive advertising developed almost to a science, and credit easier to come by than ever, it's no wonder that we have become addicted to consuming for the last several decades. We are so used to having "stuff" that we forget the lessons that our parents and grandparents took for granted.

Before the 1960s and 1970s, very few people carried large amounts of debt other than their home mortgage. People saved for what they wanted, and did without whatever they couldn't pay cash for. By today's standards, the average person just a couple of generations ago lived in poverty, because he or she didn't have a large amount of possessions.

Since the explosion of television and other media, however, we have been convinced by advertisers that we need their products. Advertising agencies employ psychologists to help them manipulate consumer behavior. As with our earlier statements about financial institutions (they may not be your friends), advertising agencies have their own interests at heart. Your wellbeing is not important to them.

As a result, we have become convinced that we always need *more*. We have to smell better, dress better, drive bigger and shinier cars, have whiter teeth—and the company doing the advertising has just what we need. The idea of consumers being satisfied with a simpler life and saving money terrifies advertisers.

The need for more "stuff" is never satisfied. We have now been conditioned to always have an appetite for the next new toy. This appetite sometimes turns deadly. A Wal-Mart security guard was trampled to death by shoppers eager to get bargains during a recent Christmas shopping season. Do you need a better illustration of how advertisers and retailers have twisted our minds so that the need for consumption even overrides safety?

This is the mentality that you have to escape. Refuse to be manipulated by societal forces that try to control your behavior for their own benefit. It's easy to deny that you would do anything as hideous as what occurred at the Wal-Mart store. When you think about it, though, have you reduced your quality of life and that of your family by taking on unneeded debt?

Quality of life is a nebulous phrase that defies an exact definition, yet each of us understands what it means. One thing is sure: when you are buried in debt and worried about how you're going to pay your bills, your quality of life suffers. Children can get over not having the latest shiny object that's advertised on television, but they suffer horribly when they see their parents in a constant state of anxiety.

Make a commitment to trim your appetite for possessions, and concentrate on your true needs. When you have acknowledged that much of what you consider necessities are in fact luxuries, you will find many ways that your expenses can be reduced. If you follow the advice I gave earlier in the book, you keep track of your expenses to make sure that you don't have any "leaks" that drain your money away.

You may decide to get rid of some of the items that are causing your debt. You can work hard to pay off a loan quickly. You can sell an item to eliminate the payments. Regardless of how you do it, it's imperative that you look at your income and your expenses. If your expenses are larger than your income, you have two choices: increase your income or reduce your expenses.

Earlier, I mentioned several ways that you can reduce expenses. You are limited only by your own imagination. Does Christmas always seem to throw you into debt? Try making gifts instead of buying them. Is your grocery bill too high? Replace expensive pre-packaged foods with basics, and follow recipes that require you to make meals from scratch. You may find that your desire to reduce expenses turns into a hobby and a health regimen!

The bottom line is that you have to do whatever it takes to get your expenses under control. There are many ways to accomplish this, but it has to be done. Running a negative cash flow and going into the hole each month leads only to financial disaster.

Earn interest. Money hidden under your mattress does not earn interest. The cookie jar does not pay interest. Non-interest bearing bank accounts don't—well, you get the idea. Remember the power of compound interest that I mentioned earlier. It's one of the most effective tools at your disposal to increase your wealth.

One of the most powerful aspects of money is its ability to earn interest, but this can be good and bad. Interest can work for you (certificates of deposit and savings accounts) or work against you (credit cards and auto loans). One point to remember about interest is the "Rule of 72."

The Rule of 72 is this: Divide 72 by your interest rate, and that's the number of years it will take for your money to double. For example, $1000 invested at 12% will double in six years: $72 \div 12 = 6$. The Rule of 72 illustrates two important concepts when it comes to saving: *time* and *compound interest*.

By planning ahead, you put time to work for you. This is an easy principle to grasp. If you save $100 a month for a year, at the end of that year you will have $1200. Do that every year for six years and you will have saved $7200. The amount of money you actually contribute to a savings plan is called your *principal*.

The real benefit comes when you factor in compound interest. Compounding is the process of earning interest on interest. Look at the example of compound interest calculations above. If your interest is compounded monthly (interest is paid monthly on what you have in your account, added to the balance of your account, and then interest is paid on *that* amount), at the end of six years, instead of $7200, you will have over $10,000! That's the magic of compound interest. By saving the same amount, and earning interest on it, you've earned an extra $3000. As you can see, compound interest is a powerful financial tool.

It's vital that you start early. For example, if you invested $1000 at the birth of your child or grandchild, and earned 6% on it, using the Rule of 72, your investment will double every twelve years. When that child turns sixty-five, your one-time investment of $1000 will have grown to nearly $49,000.

Now, let's use the same example, only applying it to yourself. If you wait until you are age 40, and invest $1000 once, at age 65 you will only have about $4000. The same initial investment, yet with a shorter time frame, yields $45,000 less. Time is critical when planning ahead. That's why it's important that you start planning NOW and take action quickly. Every moment that you delay costs you money.

This same principle works against you when you incur debt. Credit card companies make their profits off of people who are ignorant of the rule of compound interest. The average credit card rate, according to one credit card monitoring service, is around 14%. If you run up a $1000 credit card bill and don't make payments, it will double in just over five years. Make the suggested minimum payment each month, and it will take years for you to pay it off. This calculation doesn't even take into consideration extra fees you might be charged.

When you realize the difference in having compound interest working *for* you rather than *against* you, you can see the huge amount of money you are losing by incurring debt rather than saving. The 14% average given above doesn't address what happens when people get behind on their bills. Credit cards often impose a penalty when you are late, with interest rates reaching almost 30%. (Following the Rule of 72, your debt will double in less than 2.5 years!)

You don't hear much about the Rule of 72 from companies that want to extend you credit. They would much rather have it working for *them* rather than working for you. Consider how frivolously we often use our credit cards, and the transient items we pay for. How many times have you charged dinner to your credit card? It's no wonder that we have become a society mired in debt.

If more people understood compound interest and the powerful effect it can have, either positive or negative, they would be more judicious in their spending. Do you *really* need to buy a hamburger on your credit card, considering that you'll be paying for it for months? Many people have done away with their credit cards all together, instead paying cash for all their purchases. It takes willpower and a certain immunity to peer pressure, but those who refuse to pay interest to credit card companies and other lenders end up keeping more of their own money.

You can see how all of the strategies start to work together. When you implement one, it becomes easier to use another. Before you know, it you are incorporating smart financial principles into all of your decisions. When you refuse to be victimized by all the advertisements for easy credit, and instead determine to use compound interest to your advantage, you are becoming financially free.

Reject destructive debt. This goes along with something mentioned earlier: your ability to comfortably repay money you borrow. If you have trouble making the payments and also taking care of ordinary expenses, the debt is destructive. Paying high interest rates on items that give you only momentary satisfaction is also destructive. Imitate those wealthy people who borrow to buy *appreciating* assets.

Protect yourself. Bad things happen to all of us. Whether it's replacing your car after an accident, repairing your home after a natural disaster, or covering yourself financially in case of a catastrophic health problem, you can be sure that a time will come when you need insurance. Look through your own insurance coverage and make sure that you and your family are protected.

Sudden accidents or unfortunate incidents and illnesses could rob you of your savings and assets. Disability, medical, life, and liability insurance are vital to a healthy financial plan. Take into consideration your individual situation to determine exactly what types of insurance are appropriate for you, and in what amounts.

While it's not pleasant to think about our own mortality, the truth is that each of us will eventually die. We can't control that. What we *can* control, however, is the financial impact our death will have on our family and loved ones. The proper amount of life insurance can make the difference between their living in dignity and their living with crippling debt that could suck them dry in the years to come.

Depending on your individual situation, choose the type of insurance that best meets your needs. You have to think in terms of both short and long term. Many people have seen their life savings drained away because they needed long term care, and didn't have insurance to cover it.

One question to ask yourself is, *who and what do I need to protect?* The answer to that question leads to others. Do you have children? How old are they? Do you have property such as real estate, or partial ownership of a business? Do you have debts that need to be paid off? How will your family replace your income if you die suddenly?

Think ahead— way ahead. Most people grow old. Smart people *plan* for growing old. You want to make sure that your freedom to make choices continues into your retirement. You do this by planning and investing in your retirement today.

Using the power of compound interest, you can put a little aside with each paycheque, and it will grow to a large amount of money. Those funds are what will sustain you financially when you decide that you no longer care to work. Investing in a retirement account is one of the wisest moves you can make with your money.

A first step is to see if your employer provides a match to any contributions you make to your retirement account. Many will match up to a certain percentage. This is to encourage you to save for your retirement. This is free money. You won't see me use that expression very often, but an employer match is one of the greatest deals available when it comes to your retirement account. Never pass it up.

Another benefit of investing in your retirement account through your employer is that employers often offer payroll deduction. Use this whenever possible. By doing so, you are following Strategy #1—you are paying yourself first.

There are a multitude of different retirement vehicles. Consult with your financial advisor to find out which one is best for you. With the variety available, you should have no trouble in choosing one that works for your particular situation.

In 1987, a survey was conducted of college freshmen, who were polled for their views on wealth. Seventy-five percent of them felt that being well-off financially was either "essential" or a "very important" goal to achieve. Seventy-one percent said that the main reason they were in college was to get a high-paying job after they graduated.

The sad part is that only 29% of those surveyed believed it was necessary to develop a meaningful philosophy of life. Achieving wealth was their only motivation. People who set out to make millions without seriously considering their philosophy of life, or carefully thinking about what career will bring them meaning and fulfillment, are destined to be disappointed.

Henry Ward Beecher once wrote, "Very few people acquire wealth in such a manner as to receive pleasure from it. As long as there is the enthusiasm of the chase, they enjoy it. But when they begin to look around and think of settling down, they find that the part by which joy enters in is dead to them. They have spent their lives in heaping up colossal piles of treasure, which stand at the end, like pyramids in the desert, holding only the dust of things."

As you plan and work to increase your wealth, keep in mind the better things in life, like relationships, values, and providing service to others. In that way, when you achieve your financial goals, you will enjoy the success more, and have someone to share that enjoyment with.

Ultimately, the wealth mindset is one that views the world as positive and full of fortune. Financial security is a tremendous boon to your life. When you control your finances, instead of letting them control you, you make the choice to enjoy life, and to live it successfully.

Here are some questions to ponder when thinking about money and wealth:

- *What beliefs do I have about money? Are they positive?*
- *Am I using or abusing debt?*
- *How much money do I need to earn to live the lifestyle I want to live?*
- *Am I providing the type of service that can earn the income I desire?*

MY PROMISE

I promise...

- to live with financial responsibility,
- to use debt to my advantage,
- to control my spending habits,
- to view building wealth as a wide-open opportunity for everyone, and
- to add value to whatever I do.

CHAPTER NINE
—Interconnectivity—

CHAPTER NINE

—*Interconnectivity*—

My son Darryl loves to surf. Living in southern Ontario, you would think he'd be stumped, but being the ingenious guy he is, he manages to surf in Lakes Ontario, Erie, and Huron. He's really good at it, too—he knows just how to hold the different parts of his body in perfect balance so that he can enjoy the full ride. All of his muscles work together to make surfing fun.

Darryl is perfectly balanced when he surfs. His muscles work in an interconnected way to help him stay on the board. Can you imagine, though, if his muscles stayed that way all the time? He wouldn't even be able to walk down the sidewalk.

We often hear people talk about the importance of "balance" in our lives. Achieving "balance" is what makes for a good life, or so we are told. But there are many different aspects of our lives, and life is often just like the waves Darryl rides on his surfboard. Conditions constantly change, and we have to adjust to new situations. How in the world can we maintain something as mysterious as balance?

It's important that we understand, first of all, that the normal image we have of "balance" —a set of scales with two perfectly-even trays—is not functional. It doesn't work in the context of achieving balance in one's life.

Instead, imagine a spoked wheel lying horizontally. In the middle, or the hub, of the wheel is a tiny point, upon which the entire wheel is balanced. An empty wheel could probably be balanced fairly easily, and would stay there indefinitely if nothing disturbed it.

However, this wheel contains all the different elements of your life: your health, your loves, your career, your relationships, and everything else. These elements lie at the rim of the wheel, at the end of each spoke.

Obviously some of these elements are more important, weigh more, than other elements. To achieve perfect balance you have to adjust all the weights, distributing them just right.

The trick is that each element changes constantly. You get a promotion at work, adding weight to your career. You have a new baby, affecting relationships and loves. Your adult child moves away from home, adjusting the weight you had there.

Because all of these elements are interconnected via the spokes and the hub, you have to keep changing the distribution of the weights in order to keep the wheel balanced.

Isn't that more like *your* life? I know it's more like mine.

The elements discussed in previous chapters were discussed separately because that's how our minds work. We find it easier to focus on one thing at a time. All of them, however, are interconnected. Balance is important, but our lives are rarely completely balanced, and when they are, it's only for an instant. Then we have to make adjustments.

What happens when your life is imbalanced? Consider the executive who works long hours at his company, earning a big paycheck. His career and finances may look great, but how do you think his relationships with his family are doing? *Imbalance.* I speak from experience here!

Because the various aspects of our lives are connected, too much focus on just one area for too long will eventually take its toll in other areas. When that happens, our lives lack healthy balance.

Of course, the descriptions I used—*too much* and *too long*—are relative terms. When a family has a new baby, it's nearly impossible for a mother to spend *too much* time and energy on an infant. (However, ask any exhausted new mother and she'll likely disagree.) A baby is important to a family, and needs a lot of care. There is almost no such thing as *too much*.

As the child grows older, though, the mother spends less and less of her time caring for it. It would be remarkably unhealthy for a mother to expend as much energy on a 20-year-old as she did when he was a newborn. This is an example of being out of balance for *too long*.

The primary thing to keep in mind is to be *aware* that an imbalance exists. Most mothers of newborns understand that they will eventually spend less time and energy caring for their child. When a big project arises at work, most people understand that it may require more time at the office, at least for a while. If you are in a softball league, a bigger part of your time will be spent practicing, until the season is over.

These imbalances are conscious decisions. Other parts of your life may suffer for a while, but the benefit from the imbalance is worth it. Moreover, the imbalance is only temporary. We make allowances for the interconnectivity of the different areas of our lives, and make the small sacrifice.

What happens when imbalance is the result of *unconscious* actions? Almost anything can happen. Your children may suddenly start having trouble in school because you're working too many hours at the office. The attention you used to give to them is gone, diverted elsewhere.

Louise Hay, author of *You Can Heal Your Life*, says that stress affects us all over. We carry anxiety around with us until it affects our minds, our heads, and our bodies. It doesn't make sense, for instance, that giving a speech in public—a basic oral exercise involving the vocal cords and the mouth—should afflict so many people with shortness of breath, upset stomach, wobbly knees, and more.

Why should such a simple physical action be a source of stress? Because we have connected the action with other fears—of public embarrassment, of performing poorly—and the fear manifests itself physically.

Think of the person you love most in the world. Think of a time when you were together and had a wonderful time. Do you feel a physical rush, as though your lungs were filled with air? Do the day's challenges seem somehow lessened?

The interconnectivity of our lives should be clear: what happens in one place affects us in others. Often the effects are subtle and hidden. To detect imbalance we have to look inside.

Where do you feel stress in your life? Work? Home? In your relationships? When do you feel the stress? When is the stress lower and when is it higher?

The key to this exercise is that you are looking *inside* for the cause, not looking *around* for someone to blame. External situations are often outside of our control, but we can control our reactions to those situations.

Often you will find that you're focusing all of your energy on what's wrong with your life. This negative outlook makes it difficult to maintain a proper balance. We tend to give more importance and energy to that which we focus on. Only looking at what's not working does two things, it adds to the stress we feel, and makes it difficult to do more of the things that *are* working.

Creating an imbalance by focusing on solely on our problems can throw our spirituality out of whack. Like any imbalance, it can negatively affect you and your appreciation of life. Life is a lovely gift, meant to be enjoyed. Unless we make room for that enjoyment, though, we feel stressed and anxious.

Often our stress comes from having compromised our belief systems, violating values that are very important to us. These decisions are usually made in moments of duress, when the situation has become so imbalanced that we resort to unethical (by our own values) solutions.

The best way I have found to regain my spiritual balance is through meditation. I have found that meditation helps me align my mind, my body, and my spirit. Looking inward on a regular basis lets me stay in tune with myself. I'm able to detect stress before it has a stranglehold on my life.

Time spent in self-reflection is time well-spent. Stay attuned to the signs of imbalance in your life. Understand that the stress you feel in one area may actually originate in another part of your life.

In her book, *A Life in Balance: Nourishing the Four Roots of True Happiness*, Kathleen Hall offers a list of activities that will help you regain the balance in your life. **Here are a few of her tips.**

- Practice daily stress reduction (meditation, yoga, and deep breathing) twice a day, for five to ten minutes.
- Exercise for at least 20 to 30 minutes, three times a week.
- Laugh as often as possible.
- Reestablish "childlike" qualities.

- Do one action a day mindfully, such as being really present when eating, showering, etc.
- Eat breakfast.
- Pray—it is an incredible source of healing.
- Remain connected socially with family and friends.
- Make time to read. Keep a journal.
- Maintain a positive outlook.
- Practice altruism and philanthropy. A generous soul lives a rich, abundant life.

As you look at that list, notice how interconnected the various activities are, with different aspects of life addressed. It's only through paying attention to the different parts of your life that you can maintain balance.

Most of all, understand that achieving "balance" in your life depends on understanding the interconnected nature of your entire life.

Here are some questions to ask yourself as you consider interconnectivity:

- Are there areas in my life that are being neglected?
- Am I making choices that negatively affect other areas of my life?
- Do I allow myself time for quiet contemplation?

MY PROMISE

I promise...

- to recognize the interconnected nature of the various roles in my life;
- to strive for the appropriate balance; and
- to regularly examine my life for sources of imbalance and stress.

CHAPTER TEN
—Nobody's Perfect All the Time—

CHAPTER TEN

—*Nobody's Perfect All the Time*—

In a perfect world, a chart of your progress toward your goal would be a smooth, ever-upward line that ended at the destination, "Success." Unfortunately, the world is not perfect, and your progress won't be that smooth. Too many factors combine to prevent solid success.

You are, after all, only human. By nature or design, we humans are imperfect. Sometimes you can make mistakes that take you all the way back to the beginning of your journey. That's frustrating, but true. If you recognize that mistakes happen, however, you can minimize the damage they do to you.

THE MYTH OF THE PERFECT PLAN

With all of the work that you've done up until now, you'd think that you would be able to see a plan through from start to finish without incident. Otherwise, you may ask, what's the point of all the work?

The answer is, because your situation would be even worse if you didn't plan. No process is ever 100% foolproof. Life is much too complex for any one person or group of people to anticipate every single possibility. If you don't believe that, then watch the movie *Apollo 13*. The brightest minds in NASA, hundreds of scientists, worked for years to put a team of astronauts on the moon, yet the mission was botched after an explosion in space. The mission at that point became simply to get the astronauts home alive.

If that type of brainpower had to scramble because of a plan gone awry, a single human being can count on the fact that a plan will have to be adjusted somewhere along the way. But why is this?

First of all, you may have the *wrong plan*. Yes, it's true that if you have established your purpose, values, vision, and mission, you are on the way to success. But this still doesn't mean that it's the right plan for you. The problem may be timing, or an incorrect reading and interpretation of a situation, or any host of errors in judgment that can happen.

Trying to execute the wrong plan can be very frustrating. It often means going back to the starting point and beginning anew. This is a fundamental change, one that requires restructuring your viewpoint and reanalyzing your priorities. Forming the wrong plan means you have been misled by some data that you took into consideration.

On the other hand, your plan may simply be *imperfect*. You may have the fundamentals down fine, but you've created a path to success that is unworkable. This is the usual reason for setbacks. We may have been overly optimistic, or perhaps counted on results that didn't materialize.

The imperfect plan is immensely more preferable than discovering you have the wrong plan. The wrong plan must be discarded and the entire process started over. The imperfect plan simply must be corrected and adjusted. The foundational elements of the imperfect plan are still valid.

Many times, a plan gets off-track because of *imperfect information*. This can be information that you obtained from an outside source, or something that you believed to be true that proved to be otherwise. Without accurate and good information, of course, it's impossible to create a perfect plan.

Why do we use imperfect information when we create our plans? Sometimes that's all that's available. We can't always wait until everything is perfect before we get started, so we go with the best information we have. When we find out otherwise, the plan becomes imperfect. We have to make adjustments and rework the plan incorporating the new information.

Sometimes plans go wrong because of our *assumptions*. Assumptions are beliefs that exist without real evidence proving their truth. We may believe that we can count on a condition in the future because of our actions, without a real cause-and-effect connection.

An assumption that has thrown a plan out-of-whack recently is the mortgage crisis in the United States, which has affected the world's financial markets and caused mass failings of investment and financial institutions. The entire mess is too incredibly complex to go into detail here, but one of the problems was that speculators expected home values to continuously rise. The prices for homes had risen for several years, sometimes to astonishing heights. Money was invested—or gambled, more accurately—based on the assumption that real estate prices would always rise.

In retrospect, of course, the tumble in real estate values and the resulting economic chaos seemed inevitable. Yet many financial experts based decisions on the idea of a never-declining housing market. This is a vivid example of an imperfect plan based on mistaken assumptions.

Closely related to mistaken assumptions, *mistaken beliefs* can throw a plan off. Many times these beliefs are the result of the programming that we have received. It may be a belief you hold about yourself and your own abilities, or about the outside world.

In either case, a mistaken belief that disrupts your plan is fundamental, and must be addressed before you can hope to make any progress. Mistaken beliefs lead you to make mistaken assumptions. If you formulate a plan based on the belief that a certain thing is true, you expect particular actions and reactions from taking steps in that plan. The wrong belief makes it impossible to anticipate the actual results of steps you take.

ARE SETBACKS INEVITABLE?

Given that we are all imperfect, and that an imperfect person can not create a perfect plan, it's tempting to answer "Yes" to that question. Setbacks are a natural and normal part of life. However, it wouldn't be true to say that setbacks are "inevitable." After all, sometimes plans go just as designed.

The answer to the question, then, must be "setbacks are not *inevitable*, but…" *Every* plan will not suffer setbacks, but the vast majority of them do. It's simply the nature of the beast. Setbacks are common enough that experienced planners prepare for them. What is inevitable is that if you make enough plans enough times, you will encounter setbacks.

Another factor that is inevitable is *change*, and change is one of the things that can upset a plan. As the saying goes, the only constant is change! Change is everywhere in our world, from the momentary shifts in a breeze that determine a sailboat's direction, to the adaptations that form the concept of evolution. We can't always predict exactly what change will occur, or how it will affect us, but we can count on change itself. When we make our plans, we base decisions and steps towards our future as we anticipate it to be. When a situation changes, at least some parts of our plan may be rendered inoperative.

If you set enough goals, setbacks become inevitable. If your major desire is to never have a setback, don't set goals. This is a major difference between people who work according to a plan, using goals, and those who simply stay busy, hoping for success.

If you never plan on attaining a certain level, you can't suffer a setback. Whatever happens, happens. It's only when you measure your progress, decide where you are and where you want to be, that you can identify a setback. If you don't care where you go, it doesn't matter in what direction you're headed.

Encountering setbacks means that you're *doing something*. President Theodore Roosevelt put it this way:

"It is not the critic that counts; not the man who points out how the strong man stumbles, or where the doer of deeds could have done them better. The credit belongs to the man who is actually in the arena, whose face is marred by dust and sweat and blood; who strives valiantly; who errs, who comes short again and again, because there is no effort without error and shortcoming..."

Over a century ago, Roosevelt recognized that those on the sidelines are the ones who criticize the mistakes others make. The doers are the ones that make things happen, and things happen only through "error and shortcoming." While no one enjoys setbacks, encountering them means that you are in motion.

Early detection can be instrumental to getting back on track. Sometimes mistakes or missteps in your plan are very subtle. At these times, logic and measurements may not be of any use. Your subconscious mind will probably know something is wrong before your conscious mind does, and it will communicate to you the only way it knows how: through your feelings.

Have you ever been engaged in a project, and begun to feel that something is wrong? You may become edgy and anxious for no reason, or start to hesitate before taking the next step. At these times, your feelings are communicating with you, telling you that something in the plan is out of alignment. Analyze your feelings when you reach this point, so you can take advantage of the subconscious mind's power to perceive things invisible to the senses.

Why do we backslide? That it's our nature as human beings to make mistakes is not very comforting when you are in the middle of your problem. Problems tend to distract you from the big picture. Losing sight of the main goal, failing to keep your "eye on the prize," will often slow you down. However, even the greatest successes in the world have involved mistakes. It may be comforting to realize that history only remembers the successes, never the failures.

Think about writers. Ernest Hemingway is considered to be one of the greatest American authors of the twentieth century. His works are used as examples in writing classes and college courses. What he's remembered for, however, is a handful of novels and short stories. These few works represent only a small part of the huge amount of stories and articles he wrote. He is remembered for the very best of his work. Without taking away from his talent or reputation, let me suggest that Hemingway wrote hundreds of thousands of words of prose that were less than great. In fact, I'm sure he wrote things that were downright awful.

Is Hemingway remembered for his bad writing? Of course not. People know him for *The Old Man and the Sea* and *For*

Whom the Bell Tolls. His style is immediately recognizable by students of literature. His mistakes and unsuccessful efforts are forgotten and ignored.

In the same way, you will be judged by your successes, not your failures. Consider Harlan Sanders, the founder of the Kentucky Fried Chicken restaurant chain. Sanders worked at several jobs as an adult, eventually opening a gas station where he served meals. Sanders developed a recipe and method of cooking chicken that became popular among locals. He was coined "Kentucky Colonel" by the governor of Kentucky, and began to present himself as "Colonel Sanders."

However, Sanders's restaurant/gas station depended on traffic for its business. When the interstate highway opened, his traffic dropped to almost nothing, destroying his business. Colonel Sanders had the idea of selling his chicken recipe to other restaurants. He used his Social Security check to finance his trips, and eventually established a chain of restaurants that we recognize today as KFC.

Colonel Sanders is not the first name that comes to mind when you think of failures. However, it wasn't until age 60 that he found lasting success, and even then, only by virtue of a government check.

As you can see, you are almost predestined to backslide and have setbacks. The most successful people in history have had setbacks, but you don't always know it from the history books. The lessons are taught on their successes.

The laws of the universe also dictate that nothing is ever as smooth as you think it should be. The ocean has waves, roads are bumpy, and human progress often slows to a crawl. Smoothness is a manmade creation, something we look for in science fiction movies and hockey rinks. Even with the best efforts however, if you look closely enough you can see that the surface of supposedly smooth objects is still pitted and rough. It's all based on your perception.

What you perceive as a "setback" may be nothing more than a change in conditions requiring you to adapt your plans. Set aside time in advance to address variations in your plan that may occur. Safety plans for buildings have more than one emergency exit because planners know that the closest exit is not always available. You can plan to have extra "emergency exits" to use when conditions change. Trying to defeat and resist change is a lesson in futility, but adapting to change and being able to use it to your advantage is within your ability.

Another aspect that you can control is your *attitude* toward change. Of course, not all changes are pleasant, and they can create setbacks, but changes also create opportunities for those who are receptive to them. If you agree with the notion that you perform better when you are happy, and less well when you're miserable, you understand why your attitude about change is important to your performance.

Many times when change is mentioned, we groan, bellyache, and do everything we can to communicate how unhappy we are at the prospect of change. What if you changed that mindset to one of excitement and anticipation, eager to see how the change affects you? If nothing else, you would eliminate the time prior to the change that you previously spent miserable. As a result, your performance will improve.

One way to control the effect change has on you is to *be ahead of the curve*. In other words, be so prepared for the change that you actually look forward to it. By approaching change in this way, you have the advantage of being both physically prepared and mentally prepared.

On the one hand, you can have materials and information available when change happens. At the same time, you can anticipate change with enthusiasm. When the change occurs, you can leap on it and use the new conditions to your advantage.

One of the factors that causes setbacks is what I have heard called, the "rubber band principle." Any time you move out of your comfort zone, you "stretch" it. The further away you go from your comfort zone, the greater the pressure to return to your original state. Like a rubber band, pressure is formed to force you back to where you were.

Once again, old programming rears its head. If our motivators are to either avoid pain or to pursue pleasure, then programming associates pain with moving out of the comfort zone. We try to fall back into old habits and routines, the same ones that got us where we are today.

The great thing about moving outside your comfort zone is that just like a rubber band, you have to stretch to fulfill your role. A rubber band is useless unless it's stretched tight around something else. Your pursuit of your goals is only complete when you are stretching against your self-imposed limits, providing the goals are challenging enough and worth the stretch.

How, then, should we view setbacks? It would be great if we could describe them as "backward progress" and feel better about them. Ultimately, though, we have to face the fact that we are further away from our goal than we were previously. At a time like that, how do you prevent yourself from falling into despair?

First of all, a setback is *feedback*. If you keep in mind that all you are getting is information, not judgment, it's easier to keep a setback in proper perspective. Everyone's heard of Thomas Edison's statement regarding his numerous unsuccessful attempts to create a practical light bulb: "I did not fail. I found ten thousand ways that didn't work."

Use errors as feedback to correct your course. It's been said that a torpedo is sent toward its target in a straight line. By the nature of the sea, the currents and shifting conditions, the torpedo must be adjusted periodically to keep it on course. It may go too far one way, and then too far another. Eventually, however, with adjustment, the torpedo reaches its target.

Your setbacks and mistakes are simply messages from the universe that you need to make adjustments. Sometimes the message is harsh and hard to accept. Regardless of how it feels at the time, however, you can either ignore the feedback or you can pay attention to it and adjust your course. This doesn't mean that you change your goal; you merely change your plan.

Besides sending the message that you need to make an adjustment, setbacks can often offer you clues on what you need to do to improve. Weak spots in your process, your product, or your approach to a matter can be more precisely pinpointed when you have the benefit of suffering a setback. That's one thing about suffering a setback: you can completely trust the information. Nothing is as convincing as the pain of a mistake you have made.

And sometimes, we need to experience the pain more than once, before we get the message! I can recall a certain lesson that I had to experience more than once, before I was willing to learn from it – and in front of an audience to boot! The message was loud and clear the second time around, and that message was to do things 'my way', just like in the song! It took some embarrassment before I realized that I don't have to use technology just because other people do. I can be comfortable and relate to people without it.

Now when equipment lets you down, and you are at the front of a room full of people, it isn't fun. But it can be funny, especially when you are in the audience! Through these experiences, I have learned an important lesson, to lighten up, not take myself so seriously. I can laugh at my many little mistakes, not reduce them, but learn from them, see the humour, have a giggle and then move on!

Laughter can reduce the stress of a situation, so that clearer heads can prevail. Sometimes enjoying a little giggle is all it takes to get everyone working together again, as a team. Sure there are times when joking and laughing is inappropriate, so use discretion. Still, a good laugh at appropriate times (and places) shared with people on your team can be the best way to learn the lesson, admit we're all human, and get things back on track, in a quick and easy-going way. As the saying goes, "Life is too short!" let's lighten up, laugh at our foibles, and then move forward.

The key to overcoming obstacles is harnessing the *force of habit*. The classic Roman poet Ovid once said, "Nothing is more powerful than habit." Habits can benefit you or they can hurt you. A habit may be what got you into the mess you're in, and habit may be what saves you.

What is habit? It's the execution of programming. If you are fortunate, your habits have been cultivated and are conscious.

Much more common, however, are habits that are based on programming from childhood or some time in the distant past. These habits are the result of someone else's decision, not yours.

Think about something as simple as when you eat dinner. Do you have to eat at the same time each night, say, 6 p.m.? Why? Is it simply a habit? If so, did you learn that habit as an adult, or do you simply eat at that time because that's what time your family ate dinner when you were a child?

Many habits are just that simple. They are based on conditions that no longer exist. A habit of doing something a particular way may or may not be useful in the present. You have to evaluate your habits and see if they serve a purpose.

There's a story of a young couple who had only been married a few months. One night the young bride was preparing a ham. Before she put the ham in the roasting pan, she carefully cut the ends off. After dinner, her husband commented on how good the meal was (a smart husband, he was) and asked about her habit of cutting the ends off the ham.

"That's the way my mother taught me," was her reply. Curious now herself, she called her mother and asked about the technique. "That's the way my mother taught me," said the young bride's mother.

The bride, now more curious than ever, called her grandmother and asked her about it. "Oh that," said the grandmother. "When I was a young bride, we didn't have a pan big enough to fit a whole ham, so I always cut off the ends to make it fit."

Sometimes we are "cutting off the ends of the ham" — following habits that may have served a purpose at one time, but are now a waste of time. Even worse, these same habits can often be detrimental, either directly working against our goals or keeping us from pursuing other activities that will help us reach the goal.

Acting without thinking is an inefficient way to conduct your life. Habits are actions that have no conscious thought behind them. Think of the times that you have done something without realizing that you were doing it. You go through the motions of personal hygiene every morning, showering, brushing your teeth, perhaps shaving. When was the last time you gave conscious thought to any of these processes? After a visit to the dentist, perhaps? Or when you changed razors?

Acting without thinking—engaging in a habit, in other words—can lead to terrible setbacks. Maybe you developed the unfortunate habit of speaking harshly to vendors. After all, you're paying *them*, so they have to put up with your actions, right? What you don't see, however, is that by indulging that habit you are creating resentment in the vendor, maybe to the point where they have favors that they could do for you, but choose not to, because of how you treat them.

Ever had a salesperson offer to expedite delivery of something that you need quickly? If you treat a salesperson poorly, you haven't. Don't expect any favors from people that you mistreat. Acting like that—perhaps an unconscious mimicking of your parents that has turned into a habit—will work against you.

As Ovid said many years ago, habit is a powerful force. Changing a habit is difficult; ask any smoker. Experts recommend that you give yourself thirty days to change a habit. That's thirty days of constant attention to the conditions that cause the habit, and consciously working to change your reaction to those conditions.

Thirty days of concentration is tremendously difficult, but that's the kind of effort necessary to change a habit. You have to overcome the emotional investment you have in the habit, the sense that the habit is the "right" way to do something.

As you can imagine, your habits can either hurt you or help you. When you suffer setbacks, it's easier to believe that they are hurting you. That's not always the case, though. If you use your conscious mind to communicate with your subconscious mind, you can create new programming and new habits.

For example, let's say that your habit of overeating has led to an unhealthy weight gain. The best way to combat obesity, say experts, is through diet and exercise. You may not ever exercise, but you see the necessity. You can develop the habit of exercising.

Imagine yourself being athletic and energetic. Dwell on the physical sensations of being healthy. Think about how exercising regularly and achieving your ideal weight will make you feel. Become emotionally invested in the new habit—the conscious decision you have made to improve your health and your life. Then, set your exercise goals, and get started.

At first you may find it extremely difficult to start exercising, especially if it's been a long time since you did it. You are overcoming inertia, and trying to gain momentum. After a few days it should become a little easier, and after a couple of weeks, easier still. After a month of exercising—remember Ovid? —you will find it easier to motivate yourself to exercise.

You can do the same with any habit that you are trying to cultivate. Habits are a part of your life, and can lead to setbacks. Either you control your habits, or your habits control you.

When you make a mistake of some kind, recognize your weakness as a human being and exercise your right to forgive yourself. That's often much harder than it sounds, and many people find themselves incapable of doing it at all. Unless you consider yourself something better than human, however, fallibility is built into your wiring. Don't dwell on what didn't work.

If you have worthy values, based on positive consequences, forgiveness is part of your outlook. If someone else hurts you, you can make the choice to forgive them. As Gandhi once said, "An eye for an eye leaves the whole world blind." Don't seek retribution against those who have committed an error that affects you.

That same spirit applies in your relationship with yourself. If you make a mistake that impedes your progress, you are merely showing signs of humanity. Forgiving yourself is a higher expression of that same humanity.

If you forgive yourself, then you can forego the pleasure of beating yourself up unnecessarily. Expressing self-criticism and punishing yourself is a waste of energy and of effort that could be put to more productive pursuits. If you amplify your errors in conversations with other people, you are doing nothing but hurting yourself further.

That's one problem with beating yourself up over an error. It tends to amplify the error. What was once a simple issue can become something more complicated and damaging simply because you are making it so. You are simply making a bad situation worse.

The common emotion of regret can drain your energy. Any time an emotion takes your mind off of reaching your goal, it is no longer useful. Regret is almost never useful. It's like an infection that can fester inside you, preventing you from doing anything productive. The problem with regret is that it does not lose strength as you indulge it. Regret seems to feed on itself, until your error takes on mythic proportions in your mind. Regret is a focus on the past, and a blindness to the possibilities of the future.

The most important aspect of self forgiveness is to realize that any mistakes you made were made by a past "you." The person in the past didn't have the benefit of the knowledge you have gained from your mistake. Learning from your mistakes is vital if you are to make progress towards success. You can go back and analyze the times you have made mistakes, even in the distant past, and forgive that version of "you."

If you do this little exercise, don't fall into the trap of feeling regret. On the contrary, forgive yourself and move on. Be grateful for the knowledge you gained from that mistake and resolve not to repeat the mistake again.

One mistake that anyone can make is the trap of *perfectionism*. Perfection is exceedingly rare, and the person who expects perfection is destined to be disappointed.

Let me make clear that there is a difference between having high expectations and perfectionism. You should always strive for excellence in whatever you do. However, being dissatisfied with anything less than perfection will inevitably lead to feelings of discouragement and lower self-worth.

One version of this type of perfectionism is having a very specific idea of what will make you happy. The more specific your idea, the less possible it is for you to actually *be* happy. Your unspoken message is: *Only this very precise combination of conditions will make me happy. If even one element is different, I can't be happy.*

Such an approach is especially damaging in relationships. If you are expecting perfect conditions in your relationships, then you are sabotaging your efforts before you even start. Relationships involve other people, and if there is one message that I have tried to make clear in this chapter, it's that human beings are imperfect. Trying to fit an inflexible template over your relationships is sure to destroy them.

When you indulge your perfectionism, you are pushing out good for perfection. In other words, you may have a result that is completely acceptable on all levels, yet reject it because it doesn't fit your narrowly-defined idea of perfection. You therefore reject a good result because it doesn't fit your template. Such a move is impractical, wasteful, and dispiriting to those around you.

The worst part of being a perfectionist is that you can never be a winner. Even with a successful result, you won't be able to resist the urge to pick at it until you are no longer happy. "Yes, but…." you'll say, until any pleasure you should derive from winning has been completely drained away.

If you have made a mistake, how do you go about correcting it and getting back on track? The first step is to recognize that you have made a mistake. Sometimes that's the most difficult part of the process. Once again, awareness plays an important role in your quest for success.

Having measurements to gauge how you are doing is useful when you want to know about a mistake quickly. Feedback from customers and partners can help. When you make an error, try to have a system in place so that you know about it as soon as possible.

After you recognize that you have made an error, accept responsibility, to others if necessary, and firstly, to yourself. If you refuse to accept responsibility for a mistake you have made, you have no choice but to play the blame game, and that is a game that has no winner. Trying to place blame on someone drains energy from your quest, and can set you back even further.

One negative aspect of the blame game is the damage that it does to relationships. You may be able to browbeat someone into admitting that a mistake was their fault, but if it was really yours, you will both know it, and the relationship may be damaged beyond repair. Once again, stay true to your values and take responsibility when it's yours to take.

Another negative emotion is anger. Even if you don't express it to other people, feeling angry can distract you from your larger goals. This goes along with the idea of self-forgiveness: there's no point in feeling anger about something that is in the past. You can adjust your attitude so that you don't make the mistake again, but anger serves no purpose after the fact.

Earlier, I emphasized the importance of persistence in your endeavors. Nowhere is it more important than when you feel like your success train is going off its tracks. Success thinkers throughout the years, from Napoleon Hill to Earl Nightingale, to a majority of them today, view persistence as vital to getting things going forward again.

Setbacks are not failure, but often the difference is made only through persistence. Napoleon Hill said, "Willpower and desire, when properly combined, make an irresistible pair. In uncounted thousands of cases, persistence has stood as the difference between success and failure. If you're to accomplish the goal you set for yourself, you must form the habit of persistence. Things will get difficult. It will seem as though there's no longer any reason to continue. Everything in you will tell you to give up, to quit trying.

It is right here that if you'll go that extra mile and keep going, the skies will clear and you will see the first signs of the abundance that is to be yours because you had the courage to persist. With persistence will come success."

The most important thing about making a mistake is that you don't compound it. Learn from your mistake and move on. You need to keep your focus on your ultimate goal; endlessly playing over what you "should" or "could" have done will only make the matter worse.

No one is ever proud about making a mistake. Consequences are sometimes so severe that it's hard not to feel negative emotions about the subject. Successful people know that you can't let an error prevent you from pursuing your ultimate goal. When you have a setback, do what you need to do to make it right. Once you have done that, you only have the future to look towards.

Here some questions to ask yourself as you consider handling setbacks.

- What habits do I have that are working against me?
- What can I do to replace those habits with ones that will work for me?
- Are there new habits that I need to adopt to ensure my success?
- Do I learn from my mistakes, or do I dwell in self-regret?

MY PROMISE

- To learn from my past, my successes, and my mistakes, so that I can keep progressing towards my optimal outcome,

- To lighten up and laugh when appropriate at my foibles so that I can move forward quickly.

CHAPTER ELEVEN
—Dealing with Success—

CHAPTER ELEVEN

—*Dealing with Success*—

I'm pretty sure that in every sport ever played, there has been a competitor who, competing against a more skillful opponent, expected to lose. But through hard work, scrappiness, and smart play, he found himself ahead in the game, and thought, "Holy cow! I'm winning!" (or words to that effect).

It's possible that when you work through the ideas and techniques in this book, you'll reach levels of success that you've previously only dreamed of. At times that success comes after hard work and slogging away at your goals. Suddenly—poof! —you've accomplished more than you might have thought possible.

It's at such times that we as human beings are susceptible to the trap known as, "I've made it." We seem to forget everything that we've learned, and every habit that we developed to get to the point of success. Success, it seems, can often be a fickle mistress.

It might help if you understand that climbing the mountain and reaching the peak is not the end of your experience. You want to celebrate such moments, of course, because rewarding yourself for doing well motivates you to continue doing well. There is always reason to celebrate an accomplishment, be it small or large, and you should always take the opportunity.

The celebrating must eventually end, though, and you are faced with one of the biggest questions anyone can face: *What's next?*

One of the major by-products of true success is that you become wiser along the way. You realize that no matter how much you may have learned, there is still much more you have to learn. The more successful you are, the more you know you have to learn. If you think you know it all, you simply don't know enough.

This means that the truly successful person commits himself to being a lifelong learner. Education may be deep: learning more about a subject with which you are already familiar. It may be wide: learning more about a subject about which you know nothing. Nonetheless, that learning will always take place when a successful person recognizes his place in the world.

Why does this learning have to happen? Because when you have worked hard to be successful, and you've stayed true to your values, you know that there is something better awaiting you, and you want to plan for it. The only way to be prepared is to acquire new knowledge and skills, and figure out a way to put them to use.

Earlier in this book, we discussed how personal growth is the art of making *possible* that which you once considered *im*possible. Robert Browning said that a man's reach should always exceed his grasp. Let me urge you now to reach higher, and grasp the impossible.

Then do it again.
And again.

ABOUT THE AUTHOR

 Vanora Spreen describes herself as a dedicated life-long learner and is committed to helping others achieve their goals. Growing up in Toronto, Ontario, Vanora studied Business Administration at Sheridan College and Management at The Schulich School of Business. Vanora began her professional career in Real Estate Sales, quickly transitioning from residential sales into recruiting then office and sales management.

Vanora's passion for helping sales people develop their business and career led her to study professional coaching. Today, Vanora helps individuals, entrepreneurs and organizations define their purpose and values, translating those ideals into achievable goals and strategies. Vanora offers one-on-one and group coaching and consulting, as well as keynote speaking.

Vanora resides in the City of Brampton with her husband Ken and their two cats, Thelma and Louise.